ONLINE
LEARNING
TODAY

ONLINE LEARNING TODAY

STRATEGIES THAT WORK

Heather Shea-Schultz &
John Fogarty

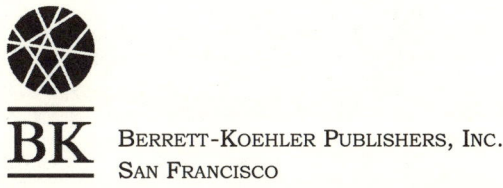

BK BERRETT-KOEHLER PUBLISHERS, INC.
SAN FRANCISCO

Berrett-Koehler Publishers, Inc.
235 Montgomery, Suite 650
San Francisco, CA 94104-2916
Tel: (415) 288-0260   Fax: (415) 362-2512   www.bkconnection.com

ORDERING INFORMATION

Quantity sales. Special discounts are available on quantity purchases by corporations, associations, and others. For details, contact the "Special Sales Department" at the Berrett-Koehler address above.

Individual sales. Berrett-Koehler publications are available through most bookstores. They can also be ordered direct from Berrett-Koehler:
Tel: (800) 929-2929; Fax: (802) 864-7626; www.bkconnection.com

Orders for college textbook/course adoption use. Please contact Berrett-Koehler: Tel: (800) 929-2929; Fax: (802) 864-7626.

Orders by U.S. trade bookstores and wholesalers. Please contact Publishers Group West, 1700 Fourth Street, Berkeley, CA 94710.
Tel: (510) 528-1444; Fax: (510) 528-3444.

Production Management: Michael Bass & Associates

Berrett-Koehler and the BK logo are registered trademarks of Berrett-Koehler Publishers, Inc.

Printed in the United States of America

Berrett-Koehler books are printed on long-lasting acid-free paper. When it is available, we choose paper that has been manufactured by environmentally responsible processes. These may include using trees grown in sustainable forests, incorporating recycled paper, minimizing chlorine in bleaching, or recycling the energy produced at the paper mill.

Library of Congress Cataloging-in-Publication Data

Shea-Schultz, Heather, 1955
    Online learning today: strategies that work / by Heather Shea-Schultz and John Fogarty
        p.   cm.
    Includes bibliographical references and index.
    ISBN 1-57675-143-0
    1. Internet in education.   2. Computer-assisted instruction.
    3. Employees—Training of—Computer-assisted instruction.
    I. Fogarty, John, 1958. II. Title.
    LB1044.87 .853 2002
    371.33′4—dc21

          2002018377

First Edition
07 06 05 04 03 02   10 9 8 7 6 5 4 3 2 1

To
Thomas James Schultz,
Cara N. Fogarty,
and Sherry L. Weiglein

Contents

Preface

Online learning, e-learning, webucation—whatever you want to call it, the fiery marriage of education and the Internet has permanently altered the way we live, work, train, and learn today. Moreover, online learning and its related technologies have had a profound effect on the way we do business—in America and around the world. Yet, to date, only a handful of business books have addressed the new opportunities or attempted to guide the interested professional in how to use them.

We wrote *Online Learning Today: Strategies That Work* for one purpose: to help those involved in the leadership, design, and delivery of online learning to chart a course through the often turbulent sea of e-learning today. Our target audience includes human resource managers, information technologies professionals, chief learning officers, trainers, educators, content designers, technology and service providers, and anyone else trying to navigate their way through the whitewater.

Thanks to the scores of training and design professionals, HR managers, CEOs, CLOs, IT pros, and providers we studied and interviewed, this book is far more than the brainchild of two authors working in the field. It is a snapshot of the e-learning industry at the beginning of the twenty-first century, including all the major players and personalities. As such, *Online Learning Today* is actually a collaborative effort, a reflection of all the time and toil that online learning professionals like you and those studied here have contributed.

The result? That's for you to decide. What you're holding in your hands right now is the fruit of over four years of research, interviews, and personal and professional experience (not to mention the endless hours of taking or developing e-learning programs ourselves). We tracked down those organizations and people who are making e-learning work today. We studied them and their methods, technologies, and strategies. We weeded out the fads, the hype, and the maybes to distill *seven core strategies* that will help your online learning work today and in the foreseeable future:

1. **Cater to the Learner.** Your success depends on the learner actually using the learning and improving from it; all else is secondary.

2. **Achieve Buy-in.** Make the business case for e-learning to executive leadership and win their commitment. Also, achieve buy-in throughout the enterprise and from all stakeholders by communicating and promoting the new opportunities.

3. **Save Time and Money.** Take advantage of the built-in time/money savings. The same two benefits that rocketed e-learning around the globe in boom times are even more important in a slower economy—as long as it makes sense.

4. **Tame the Technology.** You, your staff, trainers, and learners *must* be comfortable with the technology. You can beat technophobia.

5. **Orchestrate the Three Sides of Design.** Take into account the learning, aesthetic, and technological design factors of each e-learning module, course, or curriculum. All three must work together in harmony for attractive and effective online learning, or it will be a crash course.

6. **Think Globally; Learn Locally.** News flash: English speakers no longer comprise the majority of Internet users. When designing or delivering e-learning to international audiences, be sure you're familiar with every nuance of their language, culture, and customs.

7. **Partner with Purpose and Passion.** Partner with outside vendors strategically, intelligently, and with commitment. Also, avoid accidental and porcupine partnerships.

Furthermore, we arranged these seven strategies into seven chapters, each with a logical, consistent structure:

1. Each chapter begins with a case study that highlights the strategy addressed.
2. We follow with a list of bulleted points culled from our case study and research.
3. We then discuss those points, drawing out meaning and insight from actual, real-world examples.

We are passionate about learning online, what it is and what it can be. We have seen some brilliant starts and bizarre mishaps. As a result, we early on decided to avoid emphasizing the ever-changing technologies and instead focus on solid, core *business* strategies for their use. Technology, statistics, and data will change; the strategies are foundational. Whether it's e-learning, e-commerce, e-communicating, or knowledge management, these strategies apply. Our focus, however, is on training and learning online.

The implications of online learning throughout our lives are boundless. We adults see it as an uncharted discipline; our children see it as day-to-day reality. Coauthor Heather Shea-Schultz and her family spend a month each year in Kenya installing used American computers—technology we take for granted. Kenyans and others new to the arena see computers and knowledge as their future.

All told, we present seven strategies, seven case studies, and seven solid solutions for success in online learning today. We believe it has the information you need, and we hope you'll enjoy learning it.

Heather Shea-Schultz
John Fogarty

Acknowledgements

First, a huge thank-you to the fabulous staff of Berrett-Koehler Publishers, who gave us the vision and guidance to complete this work. Finding a publisher who will nurture (and nursemaid) a project like this is a once-in-a-lifetime shot for most writers. Thanks, all.

We would also like to acknowledge the help and patience of those scores of e-learning professionals we studied, interviewed, and badgered in order to write this book. Space doesn't permit us to list the scores of people we talked to here, so a partial list will have to do (please see the bibliography, where we acknowledge fifty-two of them). Our heartfelt thanks go out to all of you.

We drew on everything we've learned from our discussions, interviews, lunches, brunches, and e-mails with you. Whenever we paraphrase or quote someone who isn't sourced in the endnotes, the information came from our interviews.

Finally, thanks go out to Tom, Bianca, Greg, Gwen, Ivy, and Portia. And to Sherry and the dogs, cats, and parrot who stood by us. Also, special thanks to Cliff and Debbie Dickinson, for their help in getting this play onto the stage. And extraspecial thanks to Chip Bell for his inspiration, knowledge, partnership, encouragement, and help in getting this play off the keyboard.

Introduction: From WOW to Now and Beyond

Education over the Internet is going to be so big it will make e-mail usage look like a rounding error.
—JOHN CHAMBERS, CEO, Cisco Systems, circa 1999

The bottom is out of this tub.
—anonymous Wall Street analyst, circa 2001

THE *E-* WAS FOR ENTROPY

The *e-* in e-learning wasn't short for *electronic* or *electric.* It was for *entropy,* which is defined as (1) the capacity of a system to undergo spontaneous change and (2) a measure of the randomness, disorder, or *chaos* in a system.

That's right—chaos. We're not being flippant. Online learning is an ever-evolving, ever-changing system. Entropy is a key consideration, one that many industry gurus and investors failed to appreciate in the past. In five short years we've gone from "Wow, e-learning is the greatest!" to the dot-com crash and beyond.

Face it: online learning isn't going away. For most of us, it's not a question of if it will work but how. The "Information Age" or "Knowledge Age" didn't disappear just because a few dot-coms did. Online learning is still the most effective way to disseminate information and enhance performance throughout the enterprise.

Even though we were already working and publishing in the field of e-learning, we wanted to learn more. Why are some organizations scoring impressive successes with online learning while others are floundering? What makes for a smart, streamlined, and effective online learning program? Ultimately, how can online learning improve employee or student performance?

We prepared this book for a specific audience: those who design and deliver online training and performance management systems. We designed this book to be both a life raft and a "How to Swim" manual. Whether you're diving into the seas of e-learning for the first time, climbing onto this life raft to pause and reflect, or thrashing about in white water, we think you will find help in the ensuing pages. Before we plunge into these waters, however, let's examine the nature of this e-ocean and how the trade winds brought us to where we are now. Often, we cannot know where we're going until we see where we have been.

So, Where Are We Now?

The amount of stored information in the world is doubling every 2.8 years—that's a lot to know. Yet, information alone is merely that: information. Sterile, static. It's when information is *put to use* that it becomes knowledge. Ah, but what kind of knowledge?

Knowledge about our customers, about our products and services, about technology, about our employees, their jobs, roles, and future needs. Knowledge. Knowledge. *Knowledge.* But how will we learn what we need to know, all we need to know, when we need to know it?

The answer is still online learning.

We define online learning as "learning via the Internet." Call it e-learning, iLearning, online training, Web-based training, or just another tool—whatever you call it, it's still here and it's here to stay. The question isn't what to call it but how to make it work. How to *put it to use.*

Actually, online learning (or e-learning) is one spoke in the knowledge management umbrella. *Knowledge management* refers to enterprise-wide storage and retrieval of archived knowledge. This includes not only digitally stored data of all sorts (documents, databases, etc.) but also the capture and archiving of the organization's entire pool of

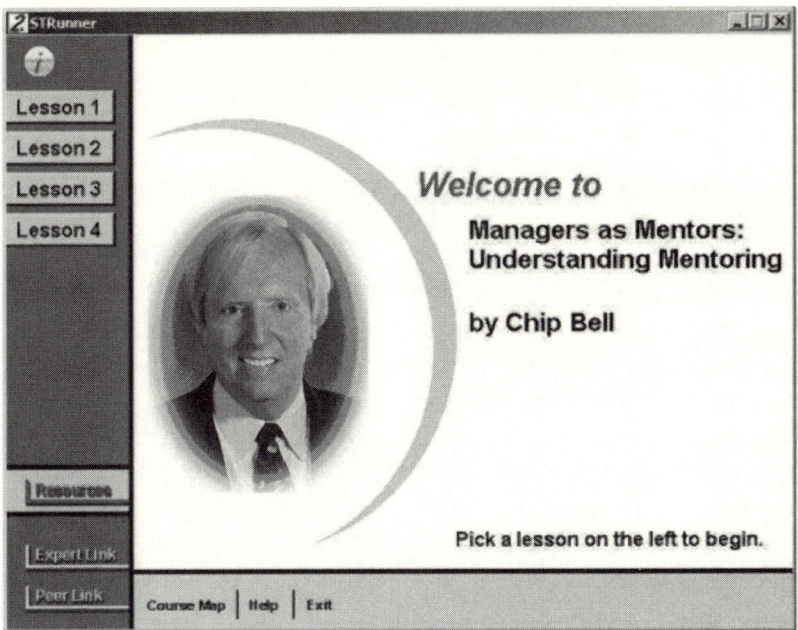

knowledge—especially the experience and expertise of individual employees.

A knowledge management system allows the entire enterprise to capture, sort, archive, retrieve, and share every jot of knowledge within the realm of the enterprise. This not only allows chunks of learning to be shared across multiple domains (which is where e-learning comes in) but also facilitates collaboration among employees, between the organization and its customers, and between the organization and its suppliers.

The ideal result of all this knowledge management? The leverage and management of intellectual capital, increased innovation, and improved performance among not only knowledge workers but the entire workforce.

Organizations of all kinds must train and educate their people, especially in our increasingly competitive global economy. Thanks to the unparalleled developments of the 1990s in computer hardware, software, and networking technology, we now have the ability to harness the vast array of information available—in many cases, information the technology itself helped generate.

The new economy, the education economy, and the digital revolution have spawned an overwhelming mass of information that is frequently difficult to access, recall, or use. And whereas information used to be a sideline to a company's business, in many cases today it *is* the company's business. But hear this: the critical and distinguishing strength of an individual, organization, or country lies in its intelligent *use of knowledge*, not the mere possession of it.

For example, Cisco Systems, the networking giant, is going ahead with plans to put 100 percent of its training online despite the tech market slump of 2000–01, and they are not alone. In Cisco's multimillion-dollar "Are you ready?" advertising campaign, a young girl states, "One day, training for every job on Earth will be available over the Internet." Is this too rosy a prediction? You decide:

- The Gartner Group predicts that 42 percent of all business e-learning initiatives will be directed at customers by 2003, up from 7 percent today.

- The University of Phoenix has become the largest private university in the United States with over sixty-one thousand students, of which nine thousand are enrolled in its distributed learning programs.

- Despite the stock market "correction" of 2000–01, online learning is still poised to consume an increasingly greater share of corporate, collegiate, and military training budgets through 2005.[1]

As our pal Tom Peters says, what was a "dog eat dog" world is now a "brain eat brain" one. In the corporate world, network technology has spurred an astonishing proliferation of educational tools that optimize investment in human capital. The goal? To provide learning solutions that facilitate the delivery of the right information and skills to the right people at the right time.

Universities and colleges are jumping online in a big way. In 2001, nearly 47 percent of U.S. colleges offered some form of distance learning, making an estimated fifty-four thousand university-level courses available online. According to International Data Corporation (IDC), almost 90 percent of U.S. colleges will offer e-learning by the end of 2004.

IDC further predicts that spending on distance learning technology for higher education will grow at a 20 percent compound annual rate, from less than $300 million in 1999 to $744 million in 2004. In addition, total investment in distance learning will reach an astounding $2.2 billion in 2004.

The factors listed in the accompanying sidebar, along with many other dynamics, have created real-world situations not easily solved by traditional education or training. Worldwide, this equates to a potential $2 trillion education and training golden egg. So what's happening now? Consider:[2]

Why this emphasis on information, delivery, and knowledge? Consider a few of the dynamics currently driving e-learning forward:

- Globalization of the economy
- Explosive growth of the Internet
- Cost containment strategies
- Shorter product cycle times
- IT vendor certification training
- Shortage of skilled workers
- Free agent mentality
- Technological changes
- Social/demographic drivers (women in the workforce and aging of the population)

- Goldman-Sachs expects the online corporate training market to grow from $1 billion in 1999 to approximately $11.5 billion by 2003.
- The United States currently spends $740 billion per year on education, more than we spend on national defense and more than the gross domestic products (GDPs) of Spain, Canada, and Brazil.
- The World Wide Web, a "toy" in 1995, is now the fastest-growing technology in history, achieving 25 percent penetration in less than seven years. Seven hundred thousand students are now taking some form of distributed learning or online course.
- Approximately 92 percent of college students have access to a PC at school. Moreover, about 55 percent of students have one in the home.

- Over 2.2 million students are expected to enroll in distributed learning classes in 2002, up from 710,000 today, representing a compound annual growth rate of 33 percent.
- Eleven percent, or fifty-five, of the Fortune 500 companies have chief knowledge or learning officers today, up from virtually none just a few years ago.
- By 2010, 79 percent of North American households will have Internet access; by 2015, that share jumps to 89 percent; and by 2020, to 98 percent.

You see? Big number. Big growth. Big opportunity. Or . . . big mess. You decide. So, just how did we get here and where do we go now?

E-learning by our definition is less than a decade old—a child. Delivering training and education over the Internet didn't get started in any formal, organized fashion until 1996. (The 'Net itself has only been around since the late 1960s and accessible to the masses only since the early 1990s.) Internet-based learning is still in its childhood, at most. Its first faltering footprints along the Information Highway (remember that term?) are still fresh in the cyberdust.

Its ancestry, however, is another matter.

We are not concerned here with distance learning or to an extent CD-ROM; we are focusing on learning delivered via the Internet (our definition of choice). Computer-based training (CBT) is much closer to the mark, as it employs e-learning's most essential tool, the computer. However, the storage and transfer of CBT content depends on the computer's disk drives, CD-ROM, or DVD—factors that curtail the amount, speed, and variety of learning. It's when CBT uses the Internet for storage, retrieval, and delivery of learning that true online learning results.

Here is the most dynamic factor: the virtually limitless amount of storage space and delivery speed provided by the 'Net. Here is where engaging, interactive, multimedia presentations pick up power, depth, and global versatility, at Internet speed, not floppy disk, hard drive, DVD, or CD-ROM transfer rates. Here is the heart of the revolution.

The Internet offers the greatest speed and flexibility for learning to date, especially as broadband access becomes ever broader, faster, and more powerful. And with DSL, cable modems, and T-1 and T-3 lines, the Internet is *always on*. It's no longer an artificial component that must be activated in order to deliver the goods. But what is this tool we call the Internet, and how did it come to impact learning?

HOW DID WE GET HERE?

How did a Department of Defense technology from the cold war era evolve into the most revolutionary learning tool in history? How did e-learning come bubbling out of the froth, and where is it heading now?

As we know, the Internet started life in the late 1960s as the Advanced Research Projects Agency Network (ARPA-NET), a U.S. Department of Defense project to create a nationwide computer network via telephone lines. The kicker is, only four computers, or nodes, were involved at the outset. The idea was that someday ARPA-NET could survive a nuclear war or other disaster because it would be stored on thousands of different computers, not one. As is so often the case, war (or the preparation for war) led to technological advancement.

During the next two decades, the network evolved into something quite different from its designers' intent. It became the province of academic institutions, scientists, and government employees engaged in research and communications. Why? Because the Internet allowed academics to connect to each others' computers via telephone lines and share data. (*Ah, here's where it starts. . . .*) It also allowed them to communicate with each other rapidly and inexpensively via electronic mail (e-mail). Researchers, NASA scientists, and others found it a convenient way to share knowledge and stay in touch. (*Knowledge . . . convenience . . . rapid and inexpensive. Hmmm. Sounds familiar somehow.*)

The only problem was a *lack of standards*. And where there are no standards, there is no compatibility. This standards/compatibility gap is the inherent weakness, the "bad gene" passed down from the early days of the Internet to online learning today (which we will address in a moment, trust us). First, let's take a look at how programmers solved the standards/compatibility gap on the Internet itself and the monumental breakthroughs that resulted.

As the 'Net began to spread around the world, users found that they were often unable to share files or access certain sites. Although the Internet connected thousands of computers by the late 1970s, it didn't account for all the different operating systems—Macintosh, DOS, Windows, Unix, and so forth. Each stored files in different and often incompatible formats. Graphics created on one computer couldn't always be viewed on other computers; video or audio files stored on a Mac couldn't be seen or heard on a PC with DOS. Enter the World Wide Web.

In 1989, Tim Berners-Lee led a team at Switzerland's European Particle Physics Laboratory (CERN) in developing what he dubbed World Wide Web standards. The most important of these was the use of hypertext markup language (html). Hypertext is the "hot spot" of an online document, usually underlined or blue or both. When selected, hypertext takes the user to a related or "linked" document. For example, if a botanist were reading a Web page about mushrooms and selected the hypertext word *psilocybin,* he or she would go directly to a document (stored on another computer perhaps thousands of miles away) dealing with that type of mushroom. If this sounds dry and academic, remember that the Web was originally conceived as a way for physicists to share research data.

Thus, for the first two decades of its existence, the Internet was fairly drab; no more than several thousand users worldwide bothered with it. Despite the use of hypertext, Web pages were uniformly dull and text-heavy and contained few, if any, multimedia effects. They were dry as chalk dust on a blackboard.

The next great innovation for the Web came in 1992, when programmers from the National Center for Supercomputing Applications (NCSA) at the University of Illinois developed the Mosaic browser, a software application that displayed not only the text of a Web document (or page) but any embedded graphic elements as well. By bringing multimedia to the Web, Mosaic pumped it full of potential.

At the same time Mosaic burst onto the scene, in 1992, the Internet took another dramatic turn. The U.S. government bailed out of network management, thus freeing it for commercial use. Swarms of opportunists moved in and began offering Internet access to the general public for the first time. Dot-coms, dot-orgs, dot-nets, and a zillion other sites began sprouting up all over the place—thanks in large part to the Web. This freeing up of the Internet from government management, combined with the new Mosaic Web browser, marked the beginning of the Internet's explosive growth.

If the Internet's explosion by itself wasn't enough to rock the world, at the same time we witnessed the meteoric rise of increasingly powerful, yet reasonably priced, personal computers, fueled by silicon microchip processors. Best of all, they veered away from bland, text-only user interfaces (DOS, etc.) and began featuring easy-to-use graphical operating systems (Macintosh, Windows, Unix, etc.).

Today, the Internet consists of several different data systems and storage areas, all of which developed independently. Some or all of them can be used to store and deliver learning. The most popular and important of these include:

- e-mail, for exchanging electronic mail messages (ubiquitous);
- the World Wide Web (www)—the be-all and end-all;
- USENET newsgroups, for posting and responding to public "bulletin board"" messages, including sound, graphics, videos, and so forth (the Internet's red-light district);
- TELNET, a way of connecting directly to computer systems on the Internet (still widely in use);
- Internet Relay Chat (IRC), a system for sending public and private messages to other users in real time (i.e., a message appears on the receiver's screen as soon as you type it; used wherever AOL does not roam);
- CU-SeeMe, a videoconferencing system that allows users to send and receive sound and pictures simultaneously over the Internet (a vestige of the early days);
- File Transfer Protocol (FTP), a system for storing and retrieving data files on large computer systems (rapidly becoming outmoded); and
- Gopher, a method of searching for various text-based Internet resources (today obsolete, like its companions Archie, Veronica, and Jughead).[3]

This combination of (1) sudden Internet power and (2) cheap personal computers has resulted in the greatest paradigm shift in the way people work, play, think, and learn in the history of humankind. If the Gutenburg printing press was an acorn from the Tree of Knowledge, the Internet is the biggest, fastest, most wildly growing limb.

So, what does all this mean for the learner or online learning in general? Why the history lesson? Simply stated, that unless the focus is on the learner, technology and content will have little impact on performance. Once the Internet adopted World Wide Web standards in order to accommodate users, Internet traffic skyrocketed. Similarly, when online training accommodates the learner (not the technology), actual learning results, usage increases, and performance improves.

The key consideration in terms of focusing on the learner, we feel, is the establishment and use of universal standards. The parallels between the need for Internet standards and the need for e-learning standards are amazingly close. In the mid-1980s, Internet users raced out to buy the latest IBM or Mac computers in order to access the 'Net, only to find they couldn't view half the pages. Similarly, in the first rush of e-learning enthusiasm, many organizations raced out to buy expensive multimedia computers, networking hardware, and Learning Management Systems (LMSs), only to find they couldn't integrate half the e-learning content they'd bought. The reason?

Lack of standards. With the Internet, it was the early users who fueled the development of standards: first the www, then the Mosaic browser (which led to Netscape and Internet Explorer), and finally multimedia Web pages designed to accommodate the browsers. These developments in the Internet are the macrocosm, the matrix by which online learning, as microcosm, may take its cue.

The Web—at first, just one small part of the Internet—has changed everything. Its development of standards, and the concomitant impact on the learning process, has given rise to a whole new world of living/learning/working/doing. E-learning isn't simply one of many resulting technologies; it's *the most profound* technology and use derived from the Internet/PC revolution.

What we are about to present is the whole picture as we see it, distilled from thousands of hours of interviews, research (both on- and offline), and personal, corporate, business experience. In other words, we are going to present the Good, the Bad, and the Gruesome. Because, just as information by itself can be either useful knowledge or static, sterile statistics, e-learning by itself can be either a razor-sharp rapier or a dull, blunt instrument—the kind butlers once used to bludgeon the victim in the library. (Can anyone say "death by PowerPoint?")

We have scoured the IT world and the business, corporate, military, and educational worlds, gathering, researching, writing, and rewriting this book to benefit our audience: those involved in the design and delivery and use of e-learning. We considered narrowing our focus strictly to end users, but since so much of what we learned will benefit designers as well, we thought it best to address both camps.

Why? Because we believe that the competent, targeted *design* and *delivery* of e-learning will become increasingly critical to the success of individuals, organizations, communities, and economies in the dawning knowledge economy. At its best (i.e., when *properly put to use*), online learning delivers opportunity, accessibility, and accountability. It allows people and organizations to keep up in a global economy that now occurs on Internet time.

WHERE ARE WE GOING?

The great need, of course, is for better-trained, better-performing employees. PricewaterhouseCoopers (PwC) states that 70 percent of the world's one thousand top-tier companies cite lack of trained employees as their *number one barrier* to sustaining growth. Despite its bumpy ride in recent years, online learning *still* offers the most attractive, cost-effective solutions to this gap.

That ride is evolving and adapting to meet new demands. Initially, IT training accounted for 85 percent of all corporate e-learning. But a shift to soft skills training has already begun. International Data Corporation (IDC) predicts that U.S. spending on soft skills training will actu-ally outpace IT training by 2003.[4]

We are also seeing a mixture of technology-meets-university/soft-skills-meets-corporate applications. This combination has already resulted in a world of odd, new, and powerful partnerships. One example is the Famous Footwear/University of Wisconsin partnership. Susan Miller, director of training for Famous Footwear, contracted with the University of Wisconsin's Learning Innovations unit to create a custom e-learning solution for new sales-people at more than eight hundred stores.

The program introduces salespeople to the culture, teaches sales skills, and trains them on the products. The online course takes the form of an interactive game in which users move around a virtual sales floor, attending to customers and asking a series of questions. Since the pro-gram takes care of the fundamental content, it frees up the managers to spend more time applying what they learned.

Such innovations are popping up all over the globe. One recent U.S. e-learning conference hosted representatives from forty-seven countries. Residents in twenty-four of the world's least developed nations, including Haiti, Rwanda, and Uganda, will receive free training through Cisco's Networking Academy on IT and networking skills.

Naturally, as online learning catches on around the world, certain fundamental problems arise. At a recent training event in Prague, middle managers logged on with glee, while senior managers couldn't understand either the technology or the English language. In the world of online learning, the generation gap is only five to ten years. The times they are a-changing.

While adding pockets of e-learning to training catalogs may be an attractive way to stick your toe in, the companies reaping the most benefits are those creating enterprise-wide strategies. All areas of the workplace, from classroom to boardroom, are seeing the shift. E-learning has sprung from the HR box and launched throughout the enterprise. Globalization, competition, and changing demographics are the drivers. Now people have access to e-learning anytime, anywhere. Or is that all the time, everywhere?

With all its ups and downs, uncertainties and surprises, online learning is still the most practical answer to providing mission-critical knowledge and skills to the extended enterprise, including employees, business partners, and customers. It has taken on a new dimension, beyond traditional education and training, to become an enterprise-/market-wide boon.

Yes, it's had a bumpy ride, but it's still big business. According to Trace Urdan, equity analyst at ThinkEquity, total U.S. revenues from e-learning are projected to continue growing from $4.2 billion in 2001 to more than $18.2 billion by 2005. This represents compound annual growth of over 50 percent (for both IT and non-IT skills training), with soft skills reaching 75 percent compounded growth. Again, that's in the corporate arena alone.[5]

Online learning is also the fastest-growing and most promising market in the education industry. Consider K–12 and university "webucation," plus educommerce (e-learning that educates consumers about products), and the numbers are staggering. Coauthor Heather Shea-Schultz points out, "My children all rely on the Internet, whether it's Bianca (age six) learning to read, Portia (eight) getting her homework assignment off the 'Net, or Greg (seventeen) taking his computer in his backpack to class and doing virtually everything virtual (homework, coaching, etc.). Yes, there is still some classroom (and lunch and sports), but nearly everything is handled online."

In the land of online learning, we ain't seen nothin' yet.

WHO'S KING OF THE CASTLE?

Content is king, say content providers (not surprisingly). No, counter others, brand is king. Without brand taking the lead, we're just another tech provider. Nay, nay, say the technical folks—forget "brand'" technology is king, queen, and jester. Still others yip that service is king. Without service, we lose our customers, and then brand, technology, content, and so forth, mean nothing. Oh, then customer is king. Or perhaps Wall Street rules—or sets the rules. So, who's right? Who's king of the e-learning castle?

Well, they're all correct—to an extent. After all, where would the content go if there was no technology? What would the e-learning customer use if there was no content? Service, brand, customer, and shareholder all go to the top. But which among these elements takes ultimate precedence? What's the most important rule to remember when designing, purchasing, or implementing an e-learning initiative in your organization? Or are we even playing by the old training/education rules anymore?

E-learning is still developing so rapidly, providers and users alike can't even agree on what it is. "Content is king," "Brand is king," "Technology is king," "Service is king," the debate rages. But all bets are off. The game is changing. Classroom walls are rearranging. New rules apply. And the first rule?

THE LEARNER RULES

None of the above—content, brand, technology, or service— is king. Only the learner is. The learner *rules*. We are so convinced of this simple truth, we've made it the first of our seven core strategies for success in online learning.

1 | Cater to the Learner

In times of change, the learner will inherit the earth while the learned are beautifully equipped for a world that no longer exists.
> —ERIC HOFFER, writer and philosopher

Everyone is the architect of their own learning.
> —APPIUS CLAUDIUS, fourth century B.C.

Never let formal education get in the way of your learning.
> —MARK TWAIN

 CASE STUDY ■ Mark Turner, GPe

When catering to the learner, you, your IT department, and your e-learning software provider must know *what* the learner needs to learn, *how* he or she needs it, and *where* and *when* they need it. A savvy chief learning officer doesn't simply have the IT department slap a million-dollar Learning Management System (LMS) in place and hope it will do the rest. You must first determine the learner's job functions, day-to-day routine, and individual requirements before throwing money around.

Mark Turner, manager of strategic alliances for GPe, a Canadian-based e-learning provider, has firsthand experience with several major players who tried just that: throwing money at the problem. Diving in with an expensive LMS without pream-ble, only to find themselves scratching their heads a few weeks later and wondering why their "e-learning program" wasn't working.

"First, we went in and looked at what they'd done," says Turner. "We then developed an entire business process model and then built the learning architecture. We were able to use that architecture to identify what technology was suitable for their business needs, rather than approaching it from the old ERP standpoint, where you bought the technology and made your business (e-learners) suit it.

"We then performed a front-end analysis of the employ-ees and their jobs, and from that we started to create the learning design. We worked with groups of employees, looked at how they did their jobs, went through their day-to-day activities, and that's what we built the learning architecture on. We knew we had to design it around each person's day-to-day role, what they are challenged by, what knowledge they felt they weren't getting, and so on. The *knowledge they lacked defined the major criteria* for identifying content and where the learning system should take them" (our emphasis).

The client (a major automobile manufacturer) is report-edly quite pleased with the results, which are still improving.

This emphasis on pinpointing the learner's day-to-day activities, roles, functions and skills (or lack thereof) can-not be overstated. This knowledge forms the major piece of the "what, how, and where they want to learn" puzzle.

STRIVE FOR LEARNER-CENTERED LEARNING

The first strategy to any successful e-learning endeavor is Cater to the Learner. Know what the learner needs to know *now*—and deliver it in the most strategically sound, individ-ualized method possible. Catering to the learner is top pri-ority, yet it often becomes lost in the shuffle. That's why we put Cater to the Learner first.

Cater to means "to provide anything wished for or needed." Simply put, you must understand why and how learners need the information or knowledge—why and how they *use* it. Is it "nice to know" or "need to know"? What level of mastery is expected? Is certification required? What's the skill difficulty? Is risk or reward involved? Are they learning solo or with others? Is the class being tracked by an LMS or graded by a teacher? Or will it be some blend of the two?

If e-learning really is anytime, anywhere (or all the time, everywhere), it can also be none of the time, nowhere—useless and *used less*. When this happens (and it happens all too often), many organizations blame the learner. *We know our training is excellent, so there must be something wrong with you people!* Learning and customer service guru Ron Zemke likens this to feeding the wrong dog food to your pooch, then blaming the dog. "When Fido refuses to eat his food, you don't fire the dog, do you? You *change the dog food!*"

It all comes down to what the learner wants and needs, and how. The key question is, *What's at stake for the learner?* It's in answering this question that we give up old ideas and begin learning anew in order to teach. Here are some steps to consider:

1. Understand *how and why* the learner rules.
2. Perform an organizational alignment to define and focus each job.
3. Identify existing knowledge/skills gaps for each job.
4. Create strategic work profiles.
5. Perform needs assessment for each individual.
6. Design prerequisite skills training.
7. Determine learning content and delivery method(s).
8. Where possible, match learning design to job function.
9. Maximize learner choice and delivery-effective programs
10. Encourage the application of new skills on the job.

Gulp! Sounds like a lot, huh? Relax. If performed correctly, these steps lead naturally from one to the next, like a row of dominoes. Actually, these are more than steps; they're just a few of the *ingredients* required for any successful e-learning recipe. Without them, your e-learning fare will be an amorphous puddle of mush on a broken plate, and your diner will starve. *With* them, you can look forward to serving up zesty dishes your learners will love, grow from, and return to time and time again. Getting hungry yet? Read on.

Based on the chapter-opening case study and our list of ingredients, let's see exactly why we should Cater to the Learner—how and why the learner rules.

Catering to the Learner

How *do* you Cater to the Learner? Quick question: How do you cater to your customers? Depends on what your customer wants or needs, right? Bearing in mind that learners are customers (and customers rule), it's time to jettison some outmoded concepts about teaching, training, and learning.

In traditional training and education, we are taught what others want us to know or replicate. The teacher controls the experience. We start at 8:05 and take a break at 10:30. We begin at the beginning of the material, and we do not skip ahead. The focus is on the materials, the technology, and the teacher, not the learner.

With an online program, however, the learner starts, stops, or skips at his or her pleasure. We go after what we need to know, when we want to know or do it. The focus is where it belongs—on the learner.

In fact, the whole idea of online training hinges on the learner—not the technology. All your efforts, technology, smarts, and marketing depend on one thing: *Will the learner use it?* In other words, "If we build it, will they come?"

Ever participate in a Webcast and wonder who is really listening? Ever wonder how many of the two hundred courses you bought have actually been watched by employees? Ever believe anyone was able to make it through the entire six-hour online course in one day? Ever try to race through an e-learning course yourself, while getting dressed?

Cater to the Learner, not the technology. This is a tough proposition for some. After all, it's technology that has made e-learning possible in the first place, right? Most of the original courseware has been in IT training, most e-learning budgets have come from IT, and most staff and people resources have come from the IT department. And what about content? Where would we be without it?

> "The average knowledge worker will outlive the average employing organization. This is the first time in history that's happened. . . . The center of gravity of higher education is shifting from the education of the young to the continuing education of adults."
>
> —PETER DRUCKER, *Business 2.0*

The learner rules, not the trainer. For some, this brings a new level of excitement: the partnership of educators, graphic designers, technical experts, and financial advisers all coming together around a new economy—the knowledge economy—with the learner in front . . . of the computer, that is.

Browse Amazon.com's Web site sometime. Everything focuses on the individual user, not the products, technology, or method of payment. The customer is king. Browse the book reviews and you'll find the Web site tailoring itself for *you* the customer, recommending similar books for *you*, read by other customers like *you*. Sure, it's smart technology, but it is unobtrusive and focused on one thing: *you*, the individual customer.

Heather recently attended the TechLearn Congress in Dublin, Ireland, sponsored by the Masie Center, a renowned e-learning think tank in Saratoga Springs, New York. To her amazement, she glanced about the auditorium and realized that, of the 387 attendees, she was one of the only ones with a training background—the rest were IT.

"Whether we like it or not, the technology that allows us to digitally communicate and collaborate is descending upon us," says Elliott Masie, industry guru and president of the Masie Center. Masie insists e-learning providers keep one simple question foremost in mind: "If we build it, will they come?"

"My worst nightmare," says Masie, "is that the techies are going to control this [online learning]. All we'll end up with is a whole lot of communication that won't give us one ounce of performance or one ounce of improvement in the quality of our lives.

"It's so easy to invent the tool," Elliott Masie says. "What we've got to do is develop the techniques, the standards, and a vision of how we can *use* the technology. We need to become advocates—not for the use of technology, but for the *proper* use of technology."[1] Otherwise, Masie warns, the new technology will simply be a more efficient means of distributing bad training.

So what is good training? Is it the what (content), is it the how (delivery), or is it the why, when, and where? Or is it *all* these? Separating these elements of online training in order to analyze them individually is like trying to separate character from plot when analyzing a novel. The elements are symbiotic, not separate pieces of the story. In e-learning, it's the what and the how that are most symbiotic, in terms of design, delivery, and effect. To prove the point, let's take a quick look at the learning process.

The Art of Learning

Real learning starts with the learner, not the teacher. People learn by solving problems, by making mistakes and correcting them, by hearing stories, by engaging multiple senses, and by following their innate curiosity. Learning doesn't have to take place in classrooms, a class doesn't have to last an hour, and motivation doesn't have to come from the threat of a ruler applied to one's knuckles. Indeed, the strongest motivation of all comes from within.

Pages, documents, classes, and files (and rulers) are anachronisms, vestiges of a bygone era of factories and smokestacks. As Alvin Toffler put it so well in *Future Shock* and *The Third Wave,* the Industrial Age has indeed given way to the Information Age.[2]

Also, realize that all learning is social. People learn what works by conversing with one another informally. E-learning gives them freedom, unstructured time, and encouragement to learn this way (rather than cramming their brains with repetitive exercises and tests). People have a need to mingle in person, discuss, and interact as in a classroom environment.

E-learning can and should meet this need. As the bandwidth pipeline opens up and organizations go toward DSL or digital cable, which creates larger bandwidth and better live audio/video hookups, learners will have not only a simulated classroom environment but also *just* the learning they want, *just* when they want it. This shift to "live" or synchronous e-learning is already spreading all over the globe.

What about specific, individual learning styles? Educational expert Howard Gardner says that differences in learning styles challenge an educational system that "assumes that everyone can learn the same materials in the same way."[3] While e-learning technology cannot determine the right method to present a particular course to an individual (yet), it does increase the odds of success by providing multiple paths for learning.

Traditional classroom delivery doesn't allow for individual learning styles—only one reason it doesn't translate well to e-learning. In the classroom model, the instructor dominates the learning process, is the primary source of knowledge, and distributes information to a class of students who study individually. Students are required to memorize facts and theories presented by the instructor or mined from assigned readings. They are then evaluated solely on their ability to regurgitate this material back to the instructor via various types of tests.

> "If one approaches an online course with the assumption that this (the traditional classroom model) is the only way students can learn, and that *this model should be reproduced online*, the opportunity for a rich and qualitatively new teaching and learning experience will be squelched."
>
> —DAVID JAFFEE, of the State University of New York's sociology department (SUNY)

We still see many trainers and educators trying to translate the magic of the classroom to the computer screen. But simply shoveling existing content onto the network is a flop. It leads to what we call "page turners"—that is, courses presented in the form of an "online book," with arrows that the learner clicks in order to travel from one Web page to the next. Sorry, folks, it's a different medium. Think about how most novels translate to movies—not very well. The screenwriter has to adapt the content to the delivery medium, not simply transfer it en masse.

Such a presentation is murder for the learning process. This, more than any other, is the leading pitfall for most on-line learning initiatives. Not only is it boring, unoriginal, and flaccid; it also fails to take into account team learning, the sight impaired, or individual learning styles that favor graphics, audio, or interactive experience.

Worse still, it's a waste of money. According to the U.S. Department of Labor, American corporations spent a whopping $63 billion training the American workforce in 2001. As IBM's executive-in-residence, Tony O'Driscoll, points out (citing similar stats for 1994), this only represents direct costs. "When time off the job is added, the total cost rises to between $200 and $300 billion (1994)," he notes. *And less than 30 percent of what people learn in training actually transfers to the job in a way that enhances performance.*"[4]

Do the math: this means that a shocking *70 percent of training dollars may be wasted,* at a time when organizations need more highly trained and high-performing personnel than ever.

"Simply putting a course or technology in place and calling it e-learning is not enough," says Keith Gallagher, publisher of *E-learning Magazine Online.* "Sure, there's an e-learning thing there, but there's no *learning* going on." Not only is the how of learning not addressed; neither is the what, which we will now attempt to remedy.

UNDERSTAND WHAT LEARNERS WANT TO LEARN

Now that we've seen how and why the learner rules, we understand better why we must Cater to the Learner. But *what*, precisely, are we going to cater? What is it learners really need to learn? Is it new behaviors or actual accomplishments that achieve the organization's goals? We suggest the latter, unashamedly taking aim at Level 4 assessment. (We'll get to Kirkpatrick's Four Levels of Training Assessment in chapter 2.) First, let's examine the what of online learning today.

WARNING: We're not going to preach measurement, ROI, and the like. What we are suggesting here is just the proverbial tip of the ice sculpture: front-end assessment. That is, before you do *any* training (e- or otherwise), you must know what you are training for. Makes sense, right? Sure. But so often we forget. Here's a little reminder. . . .

We recommend an organizational "front-end alignment," as described by Mark Turner in our case study. This is how we pinpoint areas where training may be needed. The following description focuses on training for accomplishments rather than behaviors, which we feel is the most streamlined, efficient method for targeting what the learner *needs* to learn, online or off.

As such, we find that Human Performance Technology (HPT) and e-learning are a natural fit, a marriage made in training heaven. Indeed, no less a training light than Marc Rosenberg states, "you should always take HPT into consideration as you formulate an overall learning and development strategy."[5]

A front-end alignment helps (1) determine the organization's business goals and (2) align each job toward accomplishing those goals. Think of a sculptor creating an ice sculpture of an elephant: he or she first carves away everything that is *not* elephant, then refines the sculpture from there.

Have the department manager write down his or her *business goals*. Be very clear on these, and make sure you are in complete accord. Any minor misunderstandings now will become magnified later, since the learning will be based on incorrect assumptions.

Once you define the business goals, establish a strategic profile of the ideal performance for each job under review.

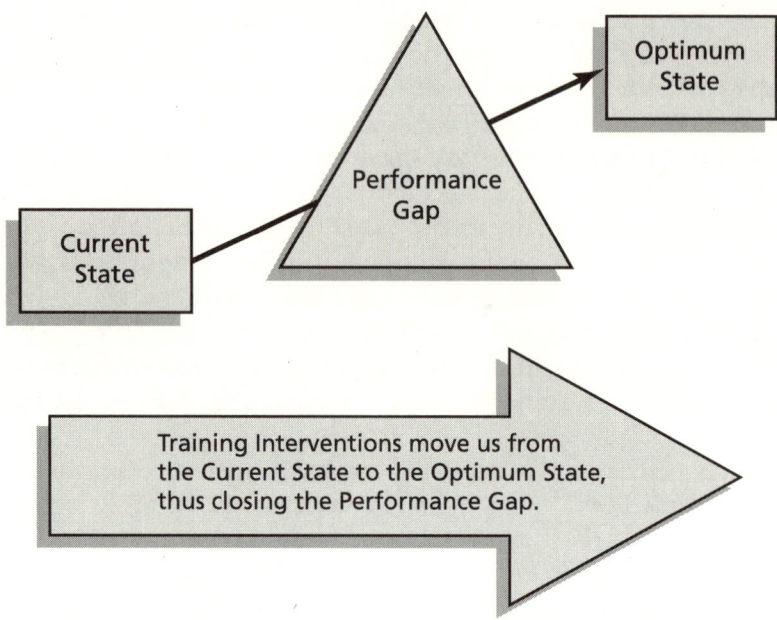

FIGURE 1.1 Closing the Gap

Ask this question: "In a perfect world, how would this job ideally accomplish the business goals?" Cut out everything that is not elephant. What you're left with is the *optimum performance state* for each job. This is the springboard from which all further training considerations begin (see figure 1.1).

Why? Because now we have the elephant. Now we can identify any discrepancies between the current state of performance and the optimum state. Notice we say *discrepancies,* not *deficiencies.* The latter applies a negative connotation to all discrepancies or gaps and implies that training is needed. Prepare yourself for a bit of blasphemy.

Training is not always needed.

Some performance gaps are not worth the cost of training interventions. Although we first focus on spotting any and *all* such discrepancies, we immediately weed out those that aren't serious enough to warrant training intervention. We focus only on those gaps that require training. How?

Cater to the Learner: ask the *learners* what knowledge or skills they feel they lack. Ask their managers as well. To quote GPe's Mark Turner, "We knew we had to design it [e-learning] around each person's day-to-day role, what they are challenged by, what knowledge they felt they weren't getting."

Next, we perform needs assessments for each job and each individual. This is unquestionably the most efficient way to refine what your learners need to learn, as well as how, why, when, and where (individual learning styles). To extend the dining metaphor, you serve your learners an appetizer of needs assessment before the main course. Be sure to account for

- stated job duties,
- actual day-to-day tasks,
- existing skills,
- learning preferences, and
- subject matter.

One of the most impressive e-learning needs assessments we have seen was designed by Samantha Chapnick, CEO of Research Dog.com,[6] a Santa Clara–based e-learning think tank. Chapnick's needs assessment encompasses the overall view of an organization, in terms of readiness to launch, support, and benefit from an e-learning initiative. It covers the gamut of both organizational and individual learner preparedness, and includes the following factors:

- Psychological
- Sociological
- Environmental
- Human resource
- Financial
- Technology
- Equipment
- Content

Multiple-choice responses are weighted with a numerical score. The response for each question is added within each category, and the total indicates an organization's readiness for e-learning in each category. Combined totals for all categories then go into the pot and yield an overall assessment of both the organization's and the employee's readiness for an e-learning initiative, course, or lesson. Chapnick is careful to point out that these categories and factors are dynamic and subject to change.

Dr. Carol Redfield, assistant director of computer science at St. Mary University, in San Antonio, Texas, agrees: "I think the idea is to give a test to see what they already know, before presenting them with tons of information. You need to determine what it is the student is having trouble with (course content, skill, etc.) and attend to that need immediately. You ask one question, rather than subject the student to an entire test."

Dr. Redfield also notes an additional bonus to this method: "By asking what a student already knows, you can eliminate a lot of redundancy in your course offering *and* make it much more flexible and personalized."

GPe's front-end work includes an analysis of the *kinds* of learners involved: those in a manufacturing environment who need hard skills training, those in management who need soft skills training, and those in IT who need IT training. "You have to identify where your training needs are most needed," says Mark Turner. "And that's usually done by identifying performance problems or areas where you think you could *improve performance that will give you a return.*" Again, this directly targets Kirkpatrick's Level 4 (see chapter 2).

The key is to ask yourself, "What is the business goal? What knowledge and skills are really needed? How are we going to develop this employee? And just how are we going to measure and assess our employees?" On the other hand, you could just slap a few hundred courses online and see what happens. . . .

OK, so we now have a grasp of *what* we're going to cater. Now we have to ask the *how*. And how to account for individual learning styles. Are we taking this "Cater to the Learner" thing too far? Big-time *no*. Because no two people learn exactly the same way.

And what if you are catering to a global audience? Think of all the possible implications for online learning. For that matter, what is this *learning* thing, anyway? Will understanding the learning process help you understand individual learning styles? Content and delivery design?

Big-time *yes*.

UNDERSTAND HOW LEARNERS WANT TO LEARN

Marcia Conner, of Learnativity, writes, "Learning can be defined as the act, process, or experience of gaining knowledge or skills. Memory defines the capacity of storing, retrieving and acting on that knowledge. Learning . . . allows us to gain new knowledge and abilities."[7]

Additionally, Conner points out that learning *strengthens the brain* by building new neural pathways and augmenting existing connections for continued learning. In other words, the more you learn, the more you are capable of learning. While children learn by building new pathways, adult brains tend to make new *arrangements* of existing sequences.

"At the neurological level," Conner writes, "established knowledge (from experience and background) appears to be made up of exceedingly intricate arrangements of cell materials, electrical charges, and chemical elements. Learning requires energy; re-learning and un-learning requires even more. We must access higher brain functions to generate the much-needed energy and unbind the old."[8]

Neurologists have long known that the sense of smell—the olfactory sense—is by far the strongest and longest retained in memory. Why? Because smell is a sense memory that readily associates itself with all others. When one remembers a favorite place, event, or person, it's often the scent of a perfume, food, or other source that summons the memory and helps maintain it.

Now is a good time to get yourself a cup of coffee.

OK, fine. So the aroma of fresh-baked cookies reminds us of our childhood. So what? What does this have to do with e-learning?

Everything. That all these neural pathways are affected by any one sense (especially smell) and form chemical associations in the brain, one sense to another, indicates that learning can be accomplished more readily by *engaging as many of the senses as possible.* This is one reason why, in days of apprenticeships, the young apprentice learned his or her trade so quickly—full sensory interaction (hands-on experience), one-on-one tutelage, and the time and means to practice what he or she learned. For our purposes here, let's focus on that first reason—full sensory interaction.

It doesn't take an education/training guru to see that full-sensory involvement in learning forges more new neural pathways—and forms more associative bonds between established ones—than simply reading text online. Are we all together on this? Good. Because now we're approaching the heart (and eyes, ears, and nose) of the matter. We're talking straight, scientific, neurophysiological differences in individual learning styles. One person learns better visually, another by reading, and yet another by listening.

The Institute for Learning Styles Research identifies no fewer than *seven* perceptual learning styles (and you thought you only had five senses?). It defines "perceptual" learning styles as "the means by which learners extract information from their surroundings through the use of their five senses." Two of these senses (visual and tactile) are involved more than once, in order to reach the magic number—seven.

According to the institute, individuals have different learning "pathways" that are specific to them. When information enters that pathway, it is retained in short-term memory. Repeated exposure and use eventually promote retention in long-term memory. The seven perceptual modes[9] (pathways) included in this theory are as follows:

Print—refers to seeing printed or written words

Aural—refers to listening

Interactive—refers to verbalization

Visual—refers to seeing visual depictions such as pictures and graphs

Haptic—refers to the sense of touch or grasp

Kinesthetic—refers to whole-body movement

Olfactory—refers to the senses of smell and taste

One may agree or disagree with the institute's findings, but that's not important here. What is important—for designers, providers, and users of e-learning—is that there are very definite and specific differences in the way people learn. Some individuals really are more "haptic" than others, while still others tend to learn better visually than audibly. The strategic question here, in terms of catering to the learner, is how to allow for these differences.

In good e-learning design, the learner can learn in the way he or she learns best—touching keys, with or without audio, visual, graphic, or any combination of multiple senses. Scratch and sniff hasn't hit the big time yet, but one program we recently sampled asks the learner first to get a cup of coffee—bringing in taste, smell, and temperature.

G. Millbank, in "Writing Multimedia Training with Integrated Simulation,"[10] studied the effectiveness of a mix of audio plus video in corporate training. When he introduced real-time interactivity, the retention rate of the trainees jumped from about 20 percent (using ordinary classroom methods) to about 75 percent.

Good for G. Millbank, right? *How do I account for individual learning styles with my e-learning program?*

Again, needs assessment is the answer—either by a human being interviewing learners beforehand or artificial intelligence subtly embedded in the course itself, shaping the e-learning as it's delivered to each individual. Either way, the individual learning styles of each learner must be determined at or near the outset. Just as you use a needs assessment to gauge *what* the learner needs, so you should use one to gauge *how* the learner needs it. This not only helps shape the content and delivery but also leads to discovering *when* and *where* the learner needs it. Is it live (synchronous), or is it Memorex (asynchronous)?

Once an assessment is made, by either humans or computers, the astute CLO or trainer will be careful to ensure that at least some baseline skills are already present in the learner(s) and the workplace. We call these the

Five Prerequisites for E-Learners/E-Learning

- Must be able to type forty words per minute
- Must have basic computer skills
- Must have access to help/support resource(s)
- Must have hardware and software that support the program
- Must have clear, compelling motivation for e-learning

Some of the biggest barriers to e-learning are as simple as lack of access to the technology and/or an inability to use it. Other barriers revolve around a lack of motivation. Unless your employees know that their jobs *require* this learning or learners have a strong desire to gain the knowledge, they may not be hungry enough to make it. The tales of unfinished online courses are legion by now.

Baseline typing, reading, and computer skills really should be a given in most organizations today. If such basic skills are lacking or insufficient, prerequisite training is in order (ingredient 6). Remember those senior managers in Prague from our introduction, who couldn't even sign onto a Web site or read English? Until that Web conference popped onto their desktops and embarrassed them, they'd never needed such a connection with computers.

> "DID YOU KNOW?
> The average online learner today is a forty-one-year-old male middle manager with a college degree seeking career advancement.

This connection is already happening with our children. Before they turn eight years of age, 86 percent of North American children will use a PC. Education is becoming *webucation*. Mom says turn off the TV and turn on your PC to do your homework. And why not? After all, the word *school* comes from the Greek *skholē*—"leisure; that in which leisure is employed; learned discussion." Learning is more effective when it's leisurely, even *fun*. The learner is more apt to stay tuned in and plugged in if it is entertaining, engaging, and interactive. That's true for learners of all ages.

Let's push on to ingredient 7: determine learning content and delivery method(s). If you've been following our list of ingredients, you have already

1. seen how and why the learner rules,
2. performed a front end analysis to align and focus each job,
3. identified existing knowledge/skills gaps for each job,
4. created strategic work profiles,
5. performed a needs assessment for each individual, and
6. designed prerequisite skills training.

As a result of which, you have

- identified accomplishments, skills, tasks, and subtasks to teach;
- determined characteristics of the learners (styles, environment, etc.); and
- established overall instructional goals.

The good news is, you've already done much of the work—and you've weeded out those performance gaps that don't warrant training. All you're left with are the performance issues that require some kind of intervention (not necessarily e-learning). Or, are you busy buying hardware, a library of one thousand courses, new infrastructure, and an LMS? Oh, you mean this is about *learning*, not technology and whizbangs and bells and whistles?

> CAUTION: Even the savviest of us still get caught up in the e-learning hokey-pokey and we forget: *Cater to the Learner*. (Is the technology even needed?)

At some point in the process, you'll get the feeling that you're setting up dominoes from phase to phase and watching them all fall into place. Much of the work required in each phase is subtly prefaced in previous phases—all aligned directly on organizational goals and all taking aim, ultimately, at bottom-line improvement.

From here, you formulate individual *learning objectives* based on your two assessments: (1) learner characteristics (styles, experience, environment) and (2) the actual accomplishments, skills, tasks, and subtasks the learners need.

Make your learning objectives concrete. Use *active verbs:* "By the end of training, learners will be able to *troubleshoot* and *diagnose* ethercard problems within ten minutes of a client phone call." Avoid the vague and general: "Learners will be familiar with ethercards."

As stated by Claire Belilos, CHIC Hospitality Consulting Services, Vancouver, British Columbia (http://www.easytrain.com), in her article "Demystifying Training Design: Writing Training Objectives," "Once you have written down the learning objective, you communicate it to the trainees and even write it down clearly on a white board, inviting comments, queries or questions."[11] *This* is learner-centered learning.

Belilos then focuses on five important points in the above learning objective:

- The training (learning) objective is performance based (emphasizing actual accomplishments on the job, not mere behaviors).

- The objective is clear and not subject to misinterpretations (learners know exactly what is expected of them and how they will be tested).

- The shift and onus for learning are on the learners themselves.

- The training lesson is action oriented (by using active verbs) that guide the learning process and later help show whether the lesson has been learned.

- The end result is observable and measurable.

Here's the magic in the marriage of accomplishment-based curriculum design and online learning: once you've set your dominoes in one phase, they begin falling into place in the next. As Belilos points out, the very *wording* of the learning objective causes you to plan training that addresses *only* those areas crucial to the learners—and the organization's goals.

So, you now have your learning objectives (based on your needs assessments, which were based on the gap analysis, which was based on the front-end alignment). Now, determining the type of learning content and delivery medium is relatively simple, based on any number of solid instructional design guidelines you already have (ISD, Gagné, Mager, Dick and Carey, etc.).

In designing the right e-learning to meet your learning objectives, remember that simplest is best. This does not mean dumping existing content onto your Intranet and shoveling it at your learners. This means identifying the most appropriate type of content and delivery media for the specific training objective, *erring on the side of less technology*. Less focus on bells and whistles, more on solid instructional design—based on learning objectives, learner styles, and organizational constraints. (We'll address specific design issues in chapter 5.)

As a guide, remember these three basic categories of learning:

- Purely cognitive (abstract and associative reasoning, processes and procedures, etc.)
- Affective: (behaviors, attitudes, feelings, etc.)
- Psychomotor (involving eye–hand skills, bodily movements, etc.)

With these areas in mind, along with your needs assessments, you begin developing the general types of learning interventions most appropriate to your learning objectives. As those objectives move from simple recall to more complex skills, select a delivery medium that will support both the learning and the skill transfer.

Just as you asked questions to determine the learners' needs, learning styles, and skills, also ask questions during the delivery selection process: "How many learners are there? Where are they located? Are they widely dispersed? Is the learning static or will it change over time?" Avoid repeating the same questions you asked in the assessment phase; our goal is to *train* these learners, not torture them.

What if you find that a skill or knowledge gap is best addressed in a classroom? Go there. What if a computer simulation is indeed the best choice but your organization can't afford it? Then do something else.

"Don't force training on the wrong media," says Lisa Collins, learning program manager for Xerox Corporation's sales education and learning organization. "Be creative and willing to try new approaches. There is no one right answer about e-learning content selection and delivery."[12]

The relevance? *Form follows function.* Try to develop and deliver e-learning in ways that support that type of learning and, when possible, the function in which it will be used. Although traditional classroom lecture is still the most common training medium, it is often ineffective, inefficient, and costly, as we have seen.

We don't want to focus on standard training methods, but we don't want to ignore them, either. We merely wish to point out that e-learning isn't always the most appropriate medium for learning. (More blasphemy!) Properly considered, online learning is just one more tool in the consultant's box. Yet, its very nature makes e-learning the tool of choice: correctly designed and delivered, it is streamlined, cost-effective, and efficient.

And within that tool of choice, you have a number of delivery media from which to choose—everything from straight onscreen "page turners" (avoid at all costs) to high-end, high-bandwidth, streaming multimedia presentations, with 3D graphics, gamelike interfaces, and all the other bells and whistles the tech wizards can cobble together. Again, the choices should be made based on (1) learner characteristics, (2) learning objectives, and (3) organizational constraints (budget, time, etc.).

Remember that delivery is symbiotic to content; the two must be considered together in order to achieve successful e-learning. Samantha Chapnick, of Research Dog, is adamant about this relationship. "Success results when the *method* of presenting content *matches* the *way* in which the skill will be used," she says. Again, form should mirror function—as in any aesthetic art. And right now e-learning is an art, not a science. Whenever possible, then, try to design the content and delivery to match the way in which they will be used on the job.

> As Dave Fallon, of Los Angeles–based e-learning provider Integrity E-learning, says, "You can't download common sense." Fitting form to function takes years of instructional design and technical experience, plus common sense. You also have to know the circumstances in which it will be used—the when and where.

What does this mean for you? That solid instructional design, professional Web expertise, IT know-how, and common sense all must come together in order for your content and delivery to mirror the job function being taught. This entails outsourcing and partnering, which we will address in chapter 7.

We believe that nearly anything can be taught online, based on our professional experience and thousands of hours of interviews, study, and research. Note we said *nearly* anything; there are some topics that simply cannot be replicated on a computer monitor—personal experience, for example, or wisdom.

UNDERSTAND WHEN AND WHERE LEARNERS WANT TO LEARN

Thus far, we've examined the what and how of e-learning. Did you notice that everything was connected by the why—including *why* we're catering to the learner in the first place? That's because we are shifting from teacher-focused to learner-focused learning—a big clue to the whens and wheres of online learning delivery.

Most of us are familiar with the term *pedagogy*,[13] meaning the art and science of teaching (especially children), often used as a synonym for *teaching*. More commonly, *pedagogy* means teacher-centered education. As David Jaffee of SUNY writes, in the pedagogic model "teachers stand at the center of all learning." Teachers decide what the content will be, how it will be delivered, when, and where.

This wasn't always the case. The great gurus of old, from Confucius to Socrates, saw learning as a process of active inquiry, not passive reception—a view that finds expression in today's adult learning theory. But something happened between the Agricultural Age and today. That something was the Industrial Age.

As Alvin Toffler points out in his landmark work *The Third Wave,* all aspects of human life were affected by the Industrial Revolution (which he dubs the "Second Wave"). In fact, says Toffler, all human institutions—including education—began to adopt many aspects of that characteristic industrial institution, the factory.

> "Schools, hospitals, prisons, government and other organizations thus took on many of its characteristics—its division of labor, its hierarchical structure, and its metallic impersonality.
>
> Even in the Arts we find some of the principles of the factory. Instead of working for a patron, as was customary during the long reign of agricultural civilizations (the First Wave), musicians, artists, composers and writers were increasingly thrown on the mercies of the market-place. More and more they turned out products for anonymous consumers. *And as this shift occurred in every Second Wave country, the very structure of artistic production changed.*[14]" (our emphasis)

Toffler goes on to describe how the modern symphonic orchestra evolved from smaller chamber groups as a response to the industrial demands of bigger, louder, more. Not only did orchestras begin to mimic factory-style production methods (division of labor, hierarchical management, etc.), but even the structure and content of the music itself changed to meet the demands of the Industrial Age (trainers, take note).

Industrial Age educational methods also conformed to the impersonal, mass production factory model. Teachers began to seem more like factory managers, while students began to mirror employees. Also, schools were built in central locations so students could come to where the learning was housed. Distance was death to the would-be student.

Not anymore. The Information Age changes all that. To use our "Cater to the Learner" metaphor, no longer does the diner come to a mess hall for standardized fare at a regularly scheduled time. Now, the restaurant comes to the diner when he or she wants it. Catering the knowledge is built into the model. And the instructor waits on the student/diner.

Now the when and where of e-learning become more discernible. A comparison of Industrial Age learning versus Information Age[15] learning makes them even more so:

Industrial Age Learning	*Information Age Learning*
Uniformity and conformity	Diversity and individuality
Memorization and repetition	Discovery and experience
Content learning	Process learning of quality content
Departmentalized learning	Interdisciplinary learning
Static and rigid processes	Creative and intuitive processes
Isolated teaching environments	Collaborative environments
Technology as an isolated tool	Technology as an integral tool
Restricted use of facilities	Flexible use of facilities
Autonomy of the community	Community collaboration

Unfortunately, few educators or school systems have paid heed to the changing times. Children continue to be indoctrinated, as opposed to being allowed to learn. Molded, packed, stamped, and stacked, like prefab humans on an assembly line. Fodder for the machine. Sadly, this factory-line model is still the norm in public education today, where social engineering has taken the place of actual learning. Perhaps that's one reason home schooling has become so popular. And more and more parents are logging on as they embrace their roles as at-home teachers.

Adult education, too, fell victim to Industrial Age, teacher-centered models. In 1926, the American Association for Adult Education began researching better ways to educate adults. Many educators, including Eduard C. Lindeman, felt that the American academic system had grown in "reverse order." Lindeman noted that subjects and teachers constituted the starting point, while learners were secondary. He believed that adults learned by what they did and that experience was the adult learner's "living textbook."[16]

Unfortunately, only some of Lindeman's theories have seeped into modern classrooms. Today, most formal education still centers on the teacher, who, though well meaning, can still stifle the learning process by dominating the environment. By adulthood, most people view learning as somewhat akin to having a tooth pulled.

In 1973, Malcolm Knowles published the book *The Adult Learner: A Neglected Species*[17] in which he states that adults require certain learning conditions. He borrows the term *andragogy* to differentiate it from *pedagogy* and to define those conditions. Since then, the term *andragogy* has taken on a broader meaning. Today, the andragogic model presents five issues to be considered in formal learning:

- Letting learners know why something is important to learn
- Showing learners how to direct themselves through information
- Relating the topic to the learners' experiences
- Realizing people will not learn until they are ready and motivated
- Helping them overcome inhibitions, behaviors, and beliefs about learning

Adult-focused, learner-centered learning would seem a given in the Knowledge Age of today and tomorrow. Yet, most organizations and corporations seem oblivious to the obvious and continue shoveling training at their captive "learners," rather than accommodating them.

Wayne Hodgins, director of Worldwide Learning Strategies at Autodesk and a highly sought-after e-learning consultant, says, "We are in the 'square peg in a round hole' phase of our implementation of the innovative technologies available to us for learning. By this I mean that we are continuing to try to force everything into our traditional understanding and models of learning. Hence, we see distance learning that is mostly a replication of the familiar classroom and instructor-led training models; we see online courseware and CBT that largely replicates familiar paper structures."

Take another look at those five precepts of adult learning and ask yourself, "Is this what I get at work (or school)? Do I know why the learning or training is important to me—its relevance to my career or my life outside the office? Do I have any say in setting my own pace, or do I have to plod along with the instructor/trainer?"

Adult learners in a learner-centric environment should know why a subject is relevant, how it relates to their roles, and how to set their own pace. They should have a say in when and where they learn. And they should have plenty of choices. Learning should be a smorgasbord, not a frozen dinner.

Let's take a closer look at what it means to maximize learner choice (our ninth ingredient), especially regarding the when and where of learning. How is this different from what we are doing now? And what is the relevance for on-line learning today?

Asynchronous versus Synchronous E-Learning

Now shake; don't stir. What's the right mix? Is it better to provide online learning that folks can access anytime or perhaps a blended solution with an instructor and virtual classmates? Many vendors, trainers, and educational professionals assert that synchronous e-learning is the ideal method of delivery. For those new to the field, this means "live" or simultaneous training, receiving instruction in real time, as it is being delivered—usually by a "live" instructor or one taped and delivered "live" to an audience.

One popular form is a Webcast featuring a PowerPoint or other software presentation, broadcast to participants around the corner or around the globe. There is also "blended" learning, which features a variety of tools in combination, such as classroom, synchronous e-learning, and independent reading or field application.

Much e-learning, however, is still delivered via *asynchronous* methods—programs prewritten, with recorded or written content designed to be used at the learner's convenience or pace. Asynchronous e-learning does not occur simultaneously with creation and delivery of the training. Some examples of asynchronous e-learning include taking a self-paced course, exchanging e-mail messages with a mentor, and posting messages to a discussion group about a course topic. Most continuing education and university work is delivered in this format.

The advantages of asynchronous learning are that it is convenient, accessible, and largely self-paced. As more powerful LMSs evolve, we're also seeing the rise of "granulized" recycling—that is, small chunks of existing content being used and reused in any number of different learning applications (see chapter 5). This flexibility, combined with cognitive processor technology (used primarily in hosted databases) is simply not practical yet in synchronous delivery. But that will change as the Internet pipeline expands.

Another change will be the ease and flexibility with which one builds an online learning lesson or course from these granular objects on the fly (see the discussion of learning objects in chapter 5). Ideally, the learner will be able to choose chunks of learning and stick them together to make a fully customized, just-as-needed learning module. Wayne Hodgins, e-learning futurist for Autodesk.com, calls this the "Lego" theory. "Eventually, learning objects will be so ubiquitous that we'll all be building Lego learning blocks at our desktop," he says. This is one reason why asynchronous delivery still has advantages over "live" synchronous learning.

Heather MacPherson, of the Royal Bank, Toronto, Canada, recently performed a comparison of both methods, culled from work she completed at the Royal Bank, to help her company's internal learning consultants work through the pros and cons of synchronous versus asynchronous training. Key considerations[18] include the following:

Use synchronous methods if

- the information/learning conveyed is time-sensitive;
- immediacy of feedback is important;
- all (or most) participants will be available simultaneously.

Use asynchronous methods if

- you want deeper reflection or learning;
- real time doesn't add particular value;
- scheduling real time is impractical;
- you are using materials from previous synchronous events;
- you want "anytime, anywhere" flexibility.

This list should be posted in every IT department and read by every CLO and CIO on Earth. Certainly, as the technology continues advancing and the Internet pipeline opens up for faster and greater access, synchronous delivery will become increasingly the norm. Still, there will always be applications favoring asynchronous learning.

Because of the anonymous, solitary nature of asynchronous learning, however, some kind of interaction should be encouraged—whether it be through e-mail, groupware (Lotus Notes, etc.), message boards, or some other avenue. This interaction should take place between the learner and teacher and between the learners themselves.

As e-learning evolves, it will become more of a "blended" approach of online, classroom, and good, old-fashioned work/life application. The concept of blended learning will continue to evolve as the face of e-learning evolves. Some combination of online work with other people and processes will likely always be in the mix.

The nature of e-learning is obviously much different than traditional classroom learning—even when used as part of a conventional class. Different skills are used. Many who once employed verbal talents will need to tailor that communication for online use. This is sometimes easier for a twenty-year-old than a forty-year-old. Since most communication takes place via written messages, writing skill and the ability to put thoughts into words are paramount, and the ability to type at least forty words per minute is a must. People who have poor writing or typing skills may be at a disadvantage in an online environment.

On the other hand, having to write everything gives people a chance to think about their responses, especially in an asynchronous setting, where you do not need to respond immediately. Furthermore, one of the side effects of any class involving e-learning is plenty of practice writing, often resulting in improved communication skills. For many learners, this outcome is just as important as the subject matter, which brings us to our final ingredient: Encourage the application of new skills on the job.

All the targeted, on-time online learning on Earth won't make a byte's bit of difference if the new learning is not practiced. Reinforcing new accomplishments and behaviors is key to any learning. This should not be news to any trainer. Yet, amazingly, we still see quality learning (on- and offline) go to waste for lack of regular practice and application.

Tying incentives to increased use of new skills on the job is one way to motivate learners, but (again) the real motivation has to come from within. Challenge learners to show off their new learning. Eliminate old ways of doing things, and see that learners don't fall back on old habits.

We'll let Mark Turner have the last word on this topic: "Once we pinpoint an accomplished process, rather than an individual performer, we can develop and complement the process (synchronously or asynchronously), so performers have a better platform from which to work. If you take a top performer and put him in a bad situation or process, then that person's performance will drop. Learners want to be able to take their skills and use them properly in a given environment. This encourages the development of new skills and the desire to acquire more knowledge and skills, and you get a proactive employee rather than a reactive one."

What Works

- Know what the learner needs to know.
- Align the learning technology with the learner's needs, wants, and abilities.
- Use intelligent assessment and measurement.
- Understand learning styles.
- Be sure the learner can type.

2 | Achieve Buy-In

Learning is not compulsory—but neither is survival.
—W. Edwards Deming

Launching an e-learning initiative without employee and management support is like racing a sailboat without a crew.
—Brandon Hall

 CASE STUDY ▪ Telus, Vancouver, British Columbia

Telus, a Canadian local and long-distance telephone company, decided to take the plunge into online learning in January 1997, when the company hired senior consultant Don McIntosh. The company's director of education had waxed rhapsodic to him about a direct mandate for e-learning at the company, which had twenty-six thousand employees in more than one hundred offices across Canada. However, by the time McIntosh started work two months later, the director of education was no longer with the company, and rumor had it that he'd been axed because of his intense fervor for e-learning.

Undaunted, McIntosh went ahead with plans to implement e-learning throughout the company. "Communication in a company this size is difficult," he says. "You don't have time to evaluate the individual units that have signed up [for e-learning]." It was also tough to sell the concept of online learning to older employees (the average age being forty-nine) who are less likely to embrace change, he adds.

Then in 1999, McIntosh presented his superiors with a well-researched, convincing business case for e-learning. He showed that the company could save $3 million annually by not sending employees to Vancouver for training every year. Sure enough, later that year, a survey of supervisors and managers showed they wanted to make e-learning operational across the company. By doing his homework, researching, and presenting the business case for e-learning, McIntosh finally achieved buy-in from the company.[1]

CREATE EXECUTIVE STAKEHOLDERS

Make the Business Case for Online Learning

Anyone who has ever risked his or her hide as an organizational champion of a new initiative already knows the story: creating ripples, however laudatory, often succeeds only in rocking the boat. Being longtime swimmers in the business world, we know: be it a new product introduction, a diversity initiative, a new IT program, or whatever, organizations resist change. So . . . how do you do it? How do you get top-down commitment to your e-learning initiative? The recommendations we've distilled are as follows:

1. Make the business case for e-learning.
2. Weave online learning throughout the enterprise.
3. Publicize/communicate the new opportunities.
4. Foster a learning-friendly environment.
5. Focus on business results.
6. Tie it all together with a Learning Management System.

Launching e-learning effectively, which involves new or enhanced infrastructure, staff training, hardware, software, and course development services, usually requires spending more than is normally budgeted for training. And, like any organizational investment, there are processes and procedures that must be followed. However, you won't win the CEO's ear with standard ROI-speak. In chapter 3, "Save Time and Money," we will wallow in the ROI equation, but for now we'll just stick our toes in the water.

As Steve Griffin, vice president and chief technical officer for Eduprise.com, says, "Using online learning is not just a technical change. It also includes *organizational and behavioral change* that requires technical solutions to be accompanied by appropriate support services"[2] (our emphasis). Which, of course, means still more money.

Yet, executive commitment is paramount. No, scratch "commitment" or even "buy-in"; you've got to have *executive stakeholders* in order for your e-learning endeavor to succeed. The top brass must have an investment in its success, not merely an intellectual commitment or emotional connection. As Tom Kelly of Cisco puts it, "You must have executive *stakeholders*, not merely executive support. . . . Executive leadership must commit organizational *and* personal resources and time."

But again, how? How to create executive stakeholders?

As Brandon Hall points out, you must first *build the business case* for e-learning, showing where and how the new process will improve productivity and how it will be financed.

Primarily, this means you must "outline the benefits to the company when it moves to these new training methods,"[3] according to Hall. Note that he stresses the *benefits* to the company, not the *features* of e-learning. How will e-learning improve current productivity? Where? How much? What effect will it ultimately have on the bottom line? Employee morale? The company's esprit de corps?

We know what you're thinking: "Hmmm . . . this 'building the business case' sure sounds a lot like ROI, doesn't it?"

No, no, and again, no.

ROI ain't what it used to be, according to Jay Cross, resident guru and curmudgeon emeritus of the InternetTime Group. With the possible exception of Autodesk's visionary Wayne Hodgins, no one else on the high seas of e-learning has Cross's foresight or humor. With a prescience bordering on the clairvoyant, Cross is constantly sought out for his industry forecasts and insights.

As to ROI, Cross is typically irreverent: "ROI is a traditional financial measure, developed by DuPont, and once credited with making General Motors manageable. But it hasn't kept pace with the times. The *R* is no longer the famous bottom line, and the *I* is more likely a subscription fee than a one-time payment."[4]

Cross insists that traditional ROI matrices are an anachronism when applied to online learning. Why? Because traditional ROI has no measuring stick to distinguish a good idea from a bad one, so excellent training hits the books at the same value as bad. The trend and emphasis is on understanding business strategy and goals and how training moves the organization along. Maybe the future is ROS, *return on strategy.*

Thus, Cross discourages e-learning proponents from trying to sell e-learning via ROI talk. "Consultants relentlessly drive home this message: 'If you want to sell a big project internally, you've got to talk ROI . . . it's the language senior managers understand . . . being fluent in ROI talk enables you to position an e-learning project as an investment rather than a cost . . . it's the secret handshake that gets you into the inner circle of those who control budget dollars, et cetera and et cetera.'

"Well, it's reality-check time," Cross counters. "Talking the ROI talk won't enable you to pass yourself off as an astute businessperson. You have the same chance of passing for French with a beret and Berlitz phrase book. A little knowledge can be a dangerous

> "The majority of us are educators who truly believe in learning as a solution. This faith sometimes blinds us to the practical necessity of making a business case for our products. By this I don't mean cases premised upon learners saving more time, passing more certification tests, getting higher post assessment scores, etc. While these are all-important metrics, they are means to the real end of having a *demonstrable impact on the performance of the learner.* In other words, true Level 4 ROI data. . . . If we cannot demonstrate the value of our courses, they won't get a chance to teach."
>
> —JIM L'ALLIER, vice president of research and development, NETg

thing." Cross believes that executives making a significant business decision consider a wide range of factors and intricate potential trade-offs, such as these:

- How risks must be weighed against rewards
- How short-term aims need to be sorted from the long-term ones
- That *any* undertaking must align with strategic initiatives
- That scarce resources call for shrewd horse trading

This emphasis on Level 4 is an extremely touchy subject among most trainers and online learning professionals, who believe that the full ramifications of learning cannot be measured by any traditional means. (How would one measure increased esprit de corps, for example?) This is why most e-learning enthusiasts shy away from proving inarguable, bottom-line, Level 4 ROI and instead focus on Levels 1 or 2. Still, we wholeheartedly believe that a case can be made for Level 4 assessment.

These levels of assessment derive from the writings of Donald L. Kirkpatrick, who in 1959 defined four levels of measuring training effectiveness. The following is a sketch of the *Kirkpatrick Model:*

Level 1 **Reaction**—a measure of satisfaction ("Did I like the course?")

Level 2 **Learning**—a measure of learning ("Did I pass the test?")

Level 3 **Behavior**—a measure of behavior change ("Am I using what I learned?")

Level 4 **Results**—a measure of results ("How will this knowledge affect my organization?")

Now let's examine these levels a bit more closely:

Level 1—Reaction. This type of evaluation measures a learner's reaction to the training (i.e. how did they feel about it?). Most trainers and educators use a course critique to measure learners' subjective reactions. The result? A page filled with smiley face or sad face icons.

Level 2—Learning. This is a fancy term for a test. It measures the learner's mastery of the imparted skill or knowledge. More specifically, was the learning objective achieved? In training (as opposed to education), learning objectives are usually skill oriented, and as such, the best measure is a performance-based measure (i.e., can the learners do something now that they presumably couldn't do before the training?).

Level 3—Behavior. Just because a learner can demonstrate increased knowledge or skill is no guarantee that behavior on the job will actually change. This assessment seeks to measure actual on-the-job behavior to see whether there was a transfer of skills from the classroom to the working environment. This type of evaluation will validate whether training was the correct performance intervention to begin with, but it *falls short of being able to tie that performance to organizational goals.*

Level 4—Results. This type of evaluation is the most important yet the least conducted, primarily because of its complexity. It attempts to answer the question of whether the organization's goals were achieved as a result of training of the performers. Again, increased skill and even desired behavior on the job do not guarantee desired organizational results. Performing this type of evaluation requires an alignment of organization goals tied to specific, measurable performance. If you've done your front-end alignment and needs assessments correctly, you should find proof that the training was not only warranted but effective.

But what about those "off the balance sheet" benefits of learning? What about improved morale, enhanced skill sets, and retained talent? Such relative intangibles simply won't show up on corporate spreadsheets or databases, unless that is what you are tracking. How, then, to justify the expense associated with launching an online learning program throughout the enterprise—or even in one department?

For years, IT departments have had to justify ROI. For just as many years, the training business has been debating the value of tracking ROI. Now they merge. But what's really the issue? What is the enterprise actually tracking?

As you can see, building the business case for e-learning is far different from spouting ROI. It means focusing not only on Level 4 assessment measures but especially on nontraditional benefits, those "off the balance sheet" bonuses we've talked about. Not surprisingly, such a focus often meets with skepticism from those who don't understand e-learning.

That's why it is so important to involve those who do—again, your IT and training departments, perhaps a director or manager who's conversant or at least interested in e-learning, has skills or knowledge gaps in his employee population, and wants to do something about it. Remember, it's the line managers and supervisors who *own* any skills or knowledge problems in their ranks. Talk to them. Find out what they would like to see addressed and how. Proselytize to them the power and efficacy of e-learning. Work from the bottom up.

This is the most effective way of bringing the problem/solution to executives' attention. Start with the employee, the manager, the director, and continue up the ladder—unless you already have a ready ear in executive councils. Otherwise, climb those rungs and bring proof from those who need e-learning most, beginning at the beginning. This way, you will present the most convincing case of the *need* for an e-learning investment, and you'll create stakeholders at the top, middle, and bottom.

The investment must be seen at the top as cost justified. One example at www.brandon-hall.com is a cost/benefit analysis one company did to determine the value of switching courses from the classroom to the computer. According to brandon-hall.com, the study showed substantial savings in both student time and the organization's money.[5]

The significance? Showing those kinds of tangible benefits in tandem with the off-balance-sheet bonuses—and showing them convincingly—is the way to gain executive *buy-in*. Bringing unit managers into the discussion, presenting their take on current skills or knowledge gaps—and how e-learning can solve them—is the way to gain executive *stakeholders*.

Although online learning has planted itself in the global corporate topsoil, most executives find themselves "little more than modern-day Johnny Appleseeds, scattering people and technologies against training programs at random with the hope that one of these programs will take hold," according to Quisic's Suzanne Biegel.[5] Adding to the confusion has been the chorus of hyperbole from a growing number of eager e-learning providers, whose vague promises of "end-to-end solutions" have left executives stumbling along an e-learning path quickly run riot with weeds and without a North Star to guide them.

"Executives recognize the bottom-line economic need to create a better-skilled and better-performing workforce, but the solution to build and sustain an impactful e-learning platform has remained elusive for most. The missing ingredient from most corporate e-learning programs, however, are clear and measurable objectives and cohesive strategies to achieve their goals."

—SUZANNE BIEGEL, chief learning officer, Quisic

The situation hasn't been much better in the middle tiers of corporate America. Indeed, many middle managers frankly fail to see the value of e-learning. At best, they see it as a perk; at worst, as an intrusion on "real" work. Many view it as a misuse of time: Are these weekly Webcasts really necessary? Does this application make sense? At least classroom training got me away from the phone. . . .

"If it hasn't been communicated from senior management, and if they're not held accountable for implementing the change, it has an impact on their [middle managers'] buy-in," says Stu Tanquist, CEO of Express Learning Inc.[6]

Yet, sometimes all that's necessary is an endorsement from senior management in both word and deed, according to Jeremy Lurey, a human resources consultant at the Los Angeles office of PricewaterhouseCoopers (PwC). Lurey claims that managers often complain that they don't have the time or money to follow through on e-learning initiatives.

When that happens, says Lurey, senior management *must* step in and insist on making online learning a priority.

So much for upper and middle management commitment. What about the crew of this boat? Although the most powerful ripples of organizational motivation emanate from the top, what about the inner motivation of the rank and file? How to get them rowing with enthusiasm?

WEAVE ONLINE LEARNING THROUGHOUT THE ENTERPRISE

Obviously, once your e-learning initiative is funded, you'll have all kinds of friends. And this is the key to winning your funds: involve as many different departments as possible— IT, HR, training, marketing, finance, and so forth. The more divisions you weave your e-learning initiative into, the more funding it will receive. (And the less likely it will appear as one vast, gaping maw of red ink.) Start with the departments and divisions that will further your goals most effectively, beginning with IT, and branch out to other departments.

Grant Ricketts is vice president of business development for Saba, a leading provider of human capital development and management solutions—including one of the world's most widely used LMSs. Like Tom Kelly of Cisco, Ricketts strongly recommends forging bonds with IT and spreading out from there.

"One of the biggest problems in e-learning today is a lack of automation between departments," says Ricketts. "The result is, an organization can't consolidate knowledge or share it with the enterprise as a whole. . . . Getting IT involved at the outset is vital."

How successful is such a strategy? Industry analyst, consultant, and researcher cum laude Brandon Hall released a massive study in June 2000 called "The Benchmarking Study of Best Practices: E-Learning across the Enterprise." Hall and coauthor Jacques LeCavalier studied eleven domestic and foreign companies with significant e-learning success stories. According to their study, the companies currently reaping the most benefits are those creating *enterprise-wide* e-learning strategies. These organizations are defining how e-learning can be used by the entire workforce as a component of the overall training plan.

"Strategic, enterprise-wide implementation of e-learning typically comprises one-third to one-half of the total training budget" in these forward-thinking companies, according to Hall. This kind of interwoven delivery allows large numbers of employees to access training on their desktops when and how they need it, rather than being packed into the same classroom at the same time. This, in turn, means a far greater opportunity for online learning's two greatest benefits—savings in time and money—to have an impact.

E-learning has thus become a major part of the overall knowledge management process. What do people need to know and when? How should knowledge be shared?

Companies that have successfully adopted enterprise-wide online learning strategies have several characteristics in common. The most important (as borne out in Hall and LeCavalier's benchmarking study) is *top-management support*. Senior executives *must* appreciate e-learning as a way to meet corporate priorities and close business-critical knowledge gaps.[7] All else flows from there.

Hall advises assembling a team to implement the e-learning plan. Again, the IT network services group should be in at the beginning, to address issues of bandwidth and network compatibility. Then marketing or PR—crucial for rolling out your e-learning to the enterprise. Advance marketing support is almost as important as IT assistance. Your learners need to know about your e-learning offerings well in advance, in order to schedule their time. As Cisco's Tom Kelly advises, "Marketing is your friend; IT is your *best* friend."

John Chambers, CEO of Cisco Systems, is now famous for his remark that, ultimately, e-learning usage will make e-mail usage look like "a rounding error." We agree with Chambers, and in fact we use his quote to introduce this book. Since Chambers's comment—and Tom Kelly's arrival as VP of the e-learning solutions group—Cisco has become *the* most visible proponent for online learning in the United States. One reason is that Cisco's top brass puts its money where its mouth is. Chambers helped drive e-learning as a corporate directive *from the top down.* He is the epitome of an executive stakeholder.

One reason is the nature of Cisco's business: nearly 80 percent of all orders that come into Cisco for networking gear arrive via the Internet, according to Kelly. That provides enormous cost savings and the ability to handle much larger volumes than manual order taking. With that lesson learned, it was only the next logical step to use the power of the Internet to help train Cisco's employees—and educate its customers and partners. That's what we mean by "enterprise-wide."

Because it is an Internet networking company, Cisco pays more attention to e-learning than most other companies might. "If we were selling widgets," Kelly says, "we might not start from the bottom layer and ask questions like, 'What is the optimal network infrastructure to support an e-learning solution?'" He adds that such questions are only natural, given the nature of Cisco's business.

So, what questions should *you* be asking at your company, school, or other organization? Which areas naturally receive attention, and which go unnoticed, vis-à-vis e-learning? One of the key elements of this strategy—Achieve Buy-in—is to ask the kinds of questions that pertain to *your organizational environment.*

Internet-savvy companies like Cisco are naturally aware of the technical end of e-learning. Their need was training and education expertise—hence the arrival of Tom Kelly, and Peg Maddocks (Ph.D. in instructional design, who ramped up the e-learning initiative in Cisco's manufacturing division), and Chuck Barritt (learning content management services), and other highly skilled and talented people. Altogether, they have transformed Cisco's corporate environment from one of purely technical excellence to a hybrid of techno/training brilliance.

"We've made something like fifty new acquisitions over the last two years," says Kelly. "Our account executives and salespeople have to be up to speed and able to communicate intelligently about these new products and technologies that these acquisitions bring in—on a daily basis." What's a trainer to do?

FOSTER A LEARNING-FRIENDLY ENVIRONMENT

In Cisco's case, it meant creating an environment conducive to the rapid acquisition and dissemination of knowledge. Breaking the knowledge up into smaller, granular chunks, tagging it with metadata, and providing fast, efficient storage/retrieval were all crucial to Cisco's success. But what about the practical, day-to-day issues that impact any kind of learning—time, space, quiet, and collaboration? What about the learning environment?

We have formulated seven steps for creating a learning-friendly environment for your online learning. Many of the ideas represented here come from one-on-one interviews with industry leaders, some from listservs, and some from good old background research. Just as you can use our seven strategies in implementing online learning, so you can use these Seven Steps for Creating a Learning-Friendly Environment:

1. **Schedule e-time.** Help learners schedule uninterrupted training time—no phone, e-mail, or other distractions. Discuss schedules with their managers. Hang a sign on a learner's office door or cubicle that says, "E-learning: Do Not Disturb." Or, if they are working at home or on the road, integrate it into their day—not their personal time. (Remember personal time?)

2. **Be sure they have the tools.** Make certain the appropriate technology is available and works. Also, ensure that the e-learner knows how to access and use the program.

3. **Set realistic goals.** Help learners set reasonable goals, including specific job skills or knowledge gaps as identified during the needs assessment

phase. Help learners target goals that will challenge them but that they can realistically achieve.

4. **Chunk the learning.** In self-paced e-learning, there's no teacher setting the schedule. If learners study for extended periods, make sure they take frequent breaks. Most effective learning takes place in twenty- to thirty-minute chunks.

5. **Track the results.** Following the training, help learners compare results with previously established goals. Many organizations supply their e-learning through enterprise software platforms called Learning Management Systems (LMSs), which automate such tracking. Link rewards and career advancement to learning.

6. **Reinforce the learning.** Coach learners to reflect on what they have learned. Assist the assimilation of new material by having learners recall it frequently—after breaks and following course completion.

7. **Help them apply the learning.** To reinforce new knowledge and skills, learners should apply what they've learned *on the job*. Create real-world scenarios for using the learning. Tie incentives to the application of new skills.

Above all, e-learning must be seen as part of the individual's job. As e-learning delivery systems improve in customization and speed, learning will become just-in-time, just-as-much, and instantaneous with job performance. Until then, make sure learners organize, schedule, and use their e-learning time to best advantage. Let them know that each person is ultimately in charge of his or her own training—and career advancement.

TIE IT ALL TOGETHER WITH AN LMS

The most comprehensive way to manage everything we've discussed so far—*and achieve organizational buy-in*—is to employ a Learning Management System. An LMS is not the ultimate panacea, but you must figure out how to manage the process, like any business.

"One of the fundamental dynamics we've brought to the table is learning utilization—treating learning as a line of business," says Saba's Grant Ricketts. "Without a comprehensive LMS in place, you have a lack of automation and standardization between departments and throughout the enterprise. When you start standardizing your system and approach, however, you can start scaling it more efficiently enterprise-wide."

So, what *scales*? According to industry leaders such as Grant Ricketts, Tom Kelly, Brandon Hall, Elliott Masie, and a host of others, the answer is an LMS. With an LMS in place, you can *scale* the learning stream throughout the enterprise, from a single trickle to a rushing torrent with channels reaching every desktop. This is what separates the serious e-learning player from the dabbler—and ensures top-down organizational commitment. With an LMS in place, your company stands a much greater chance of making e-learning work successfully.

Why? Because an LMS not only tracks, measures, organizes, and customizes training for the entire organization; it also ensures consistency and buy-in. Learning Management Systems, like senior execs, don't come cheap. In for a penny, in for a pound. Once an organization makes a six- or seven-figure investment in an enterprise-wide LMS, chances are executive stakeholders will ensure top-down commitment to e-learning.

So, just what *is* a Learning Management System, anyway? And what should you look for in one?

The Nuts and Bolts of an LMS

Essentially, an LMS is the software foundation for all the e-learning in the enterprise. It provides the infrastructure and database from which employees can instantly summon a custom e-learning course, register the course, perform individual needs assessment, track progress, or simply tap a quick, just-as-much, just-in-time chunk of knowledge. Ideally, once the LMS is up and running, it can mentor, monitor, and measure the entire enterprise—including employees, customers, and vendors.

This is not the same as a Learning Content Management System (LCMS), which is a smaller, more flexible software platform for identifying and delivering small chunks of learning (reusable learning objects, etc.). As such, an LCMS can be likened to a smaller sea of learning within the ocean of an enterprise-wide LMS.

Some of the more sophisticated LMSs we've seen even cross the line from e-learning superstructure to e-commerce bean counter, monitoring payments from clients, internal billing, course registration, number of bagels ordered, or product fulfillment. They count, track, and monitor *everything*. (In fact, their omniscience is a little scary.) Obviously, this is a much bigger investment (and risk) than the application service provider (ASP) model, in which the client leaves everything up to a vendor offering a single point of access on the Web, who bills the client monthly, like a "learning utility." The problem with this approach is that you don't own anything; the vendor owns it all. And that, gentle reader, means you cannot customize it on the fly, as needs change on a day-to-day basis.

Those shopping for an e-learning platform must choose whether to lease a learning portal from an ASP and let it manage everything, or dive in with the outright purchase of a full-blown LMS. True, using a

---

ADL/SCORM: A Primer

In November 1997, the Department of Defense (DoD) and the Office of Science and Technology Policy launched the Advanced Distributed Learning (ADL) initiative. The ADL is a consortium of government, industry, and academy groups whose goal is to codify a common framework for the interoperability of learning tools and content on a global scale.

The ADL co-lab is essentially a forum for cooperative research, development, and assessment of new learning technology guidelines and specifications. This effort includes work with a number of other computer- and electronic-based standards bodies, such as the Instructional Management Systems Global Learning Consortium (IMS), the Institute of Electrical and Electronics Engineers (IEEE), and the AICC.

vendor or third-party ASP to manage your e-learning architecture is the easier choice for those in a hurry or for whom IT expertise is lacking. However, it's also more expensive in the long term, as licensing fees over the course of three to five years could exceed the cost of an LMS. On the other hand, the ASP route would delay such tough purchasing decisions while the LMS market matures, according to some analysts. More alphabet soup? We don't think so. The point is, know what you need and why. Otherwise, this tasty solution can quickly spill into a big, expensive mess.

In January 2000, ADL finally released version 1.0 of the Sharable Content Object Reference Model (SCORM). This was the first comprehensive set of standards for shared learning objects for use in e-learning. Since then, ADL has conducted several "Plugfest" events with industry, academia, the military, and international standards groups to assess the viability of the initial SCORM specification (updated to version 1.2 in January 2001). These Plugfests provide ADL partners with the opportunity to synchronize the evolution and convergence of commercial authoring tools, LMSs, and Web-based courses with the emerging open-architecture specification.

As more organizations attempt to collect, track, and manage the knowledge of their workforce, LMSs are increasingly seen as a tool that can assist with skill-gap analysis and development plans for future learning needs. They also come in handy if your industry is regulated and you must provide regular, periodic training for your employees. The ability to assess, test, and track the results of hundreds—even *thousands*—of employees is invaluable.

Ah, but not all LMSs are alike; to paraphrase George Orwell, some *are* more equal than others. And more expensive. Initial outlay for a custom LMS can range anywhere from $35,000 to over $1 million, depending on size, options, and interoperability. By "interoperability," we mean the ability to interface not only with your enterprise or ERP network and software but also with other vendors' e-learning courses. As open standards increasingly influence the creation and delivery of learning objects, having an up-to-date, standards-based LMS is crucial. Your LMS should be an open, scalable system that provides a foundation for e-learning, especially object-based e-learning (RLOs, RIOs, etc.; see chapter 5).

Any LMS you select should be AICC-certified (Aviation Industry Computer-based Training Committee), an existing standard for tracking users and test results across different courses. We also highly recommend an LMS that adheres to and supports ADL/SCORM specifications, which we project will one day be *the* standard for XML-based learning object authoring and delivery systems.

Again, Learning Management Systems don't come cheap, whether you merely lease one or buy it outright (typically, the leasing or licensing option is most common). It also can take months to complete an in-depth, enterprise e-learning analysis before implementation. However, the long-term cost savings is so substantial, the investment is well worth it—especially the investment in making sure the design is right for your organization.

Currently, thousands of various knowledge management and Learning Management Systems are on the market. In the wake of plummeting stock prices and decreased funding, however, a major shake-out began in early 2001. We believe this will result in a handful of top, brand-name LMS providers (survivors) by 2003. What to look for when shopping for your LMS? We suggest the following list:

- **Compatibility.** Your LMS should work with third-party content and authoring tools, other database-driven software, synchronous e-learning systems, ERP software, and more. (This feature is also called *interoperability*.)

- **Cost.** Pricing structures and licensing fees are complex and varied. These can range from per-use to per-employee models. Compare pricing models based on actual proposed use, and maintain your focus on the long haul.

- **IT partnership.** No matter how "intuitive" a salesperson tells you an LMS is, coordinating it with your existing enterprise management system is no mean feat.

You will need IT partnership and *buy-in*. You'll also require custom programming to integrate any LMS into the existing enterprise.

- **Market consolidation.** As the market continues shaking out, merging, and consolidating, the number of LMS vendors will shrink. Beware that most will not be around a year or two from now and that many LMSs currently in place may be outmoded by then.

Clark Aldrich, resident e-learning simulations guru at SimuLearn, has this to say about the current state of LMSs: "Content can be flopped in and out, synchronous vendors will come and go, but you live and die by your LMS," he warns. "The worst thing you can do is hurry your decision."

What Works

- Know who "owns" skills/knowledge problems.
- Communicate their need to top executives.
- Promote e-learning throughout the enterprise.
- Change the culture, not the people.
- Learn with your Learning Management System.

3 | Save Time and Money

Remember that time is money.
> —BENJAMIN FRANKLIN,
> "Advice to a Young Tradesman"

If I had six hours to chop down a tree, I'd spend the first four sharpening the axe.
> —ABRAHAM LINCOLN, noted railsplitter

 CASE STUDY ▪ IBM and Basic Blue

The computer giant IBM faced an enormous training challenge: provide thousands of managers scattered all over the globe with consistent, compelling learning in a cost-effective manner. Most IBM managers were already working ten- to twelve-hour days, so taking them off-site for additional class time was out. IBM's challenge was to provide effective learning for its managers that was practical, cost-effective, and engaging.

In 1999, IBM adopted Basic Blue for Managers, an innovative new management training program. Leveraging the power of online learning and the Lotus Learning Space management system, Basic Blue is a blended solution that combines Web-based learning, simulations, and collaboration with traditional face-to-face learning labs. By providing ongoing access to learning, Basic Blue makes training an ongoing process, not a one-time event. It also saved IBM a fortune.

According to IBM spokespeople, the results of Basic Blue are astounding, in terms of time and money savings—to say nothing of the results. IBM estimated that the per-student cost for training each manager via Basic Blue was $10.9 million for four thousand managers ($2,725 each)—a significantly lower cost than traditional classroom training. Furthermore, IBM data indicate that e-learning saved the company $16 million in 2000 alone.

To date, more than four thousand IBM managers have completed the training and given it rave reviews. Not only has the program reportedly saved IBM a total of over $200 million—$80 million on transportation alone—it actually seems to *work.*

"Basic Blue participants are definitely more prepared to be IBM managers," says Bob MacGregor, manager of management development. "They know the material better, and they know how to use it better."

CAPITALIZE ON BUILT-IN TIME/MONEY SAVINGS

At first glance, this strategy looks like yet another of those hubristic claims so gleefully tossed about in the dot-com days, regarding online learning. Save time *and* money? With better results? How?

You've heard all the stories by now: how big-name corporations are saving big-time money (and big-money time) by using e-learning over traditional training. (Caveat: we've also heard that maybe they *didn't.*) We all know, don't we, that *some* inherent cost-savings must be involved. But are all these claims for real? Does e-learning really save time *and* money?

If you can believe what the companies themselves report, the answer is a big-time yes. Organizations all over the world—including IBM, Cisco, PwC, Intel, and Charles Schwab—are saving gobs of time *and* money as the result of using e-learning. But again, *how?*

In terms of pure monetary savings, the standard reply is *travel costs*. There are none. No more sending employees out and about for weeks and weeks of training. No more hotel, meal, or "miscellaneous" costs. Now, employees get their training—even required continuing ed hours—without ever leaving their desks.

This also means *less lost productivity*. Anytime you send someone out of the office or the sales field to take training, you're losing money. Think of a salesperson who normally generates $25,000 a week in revenues suddenly being whisked away from the fields of green and cloistered in some classroom for six weeks; $150,000 isn't exactly chump change.

Then there are the time savings. Most of the organizations we studied claim dramatic improvements in time-to-train and time-to-market for their people and products when using online learning. We'll get to those numbers in a moment. First, let's examine the areas of time/money savings most commonly cited by e-learning enthusiasts: (1) no travel costs/less lost production and (2) shorter training time. For this strategy, then, our list of ingredients are basic and few:

- Take advantage of the intrinsic time/money savings of online learning.
- Measure your results, *but don't get carried away with it.*
- Broadcast success stories.
- Fine-tune your online learning as needed.

At What Price?

Think of the costs typically associated with traditional training:

- Seminar site rentals
- Instructor fees
- Books and materials
- Transportation

- Food and lodging
- Tips, trinkets, and those infamous "incidentals"

Ideally, e-learning can streamline these costs and eliminate some of them altogether—as well as recapture productivity normally lost when employees attend training sessions. This is not merely opinion but fact. The key word is *ideally*.

So where's the proof? Where is the hard data to support all these claims?

Brandon Hall's benchmarking study (introduced in the last chapter) revealed that companies realize a *40 to 60 percent cost savings* from e-learning when compared with traditional instructor-led training. Furthermore, these companies also achieved an average *reduction in training time of anywhere from 30 to 70 percent,* with the median being about 50 percent.[1] The combined savings in money and time are persuasive. And these companies are not alone.

"By 2003, 50 percent of all training may be online," according to Hall. He also states that e-learning allows organizations to "save 50 percent of the time invested in training, and cut one-third to one-half the cost."[2]

Cisco, the Silicon Valley networking giant, echoes these numbers. In addition, Cisco cites the following statistics on a Web page dedicated to e-learning trends:

- The Internet grew at a rate of 1,000 percent from 1990 to 1999 (Alta Vista and Cinnet.com).
- By 2003, only half of all IT training will be delivered via traditional instructor-led settings.
- By 2005, 53.8 percent of the market will be focused on business skills and other non-IT skills.
- The online learning market is expected to grow from about $2.3 billion in 2000 to $18 billion in 2005.[3]

Although actual percentages quoted by industry experts may vary, these numbers are fairly standard: 50 percent of all training online by 2003; training time cut by 50 percent; training costs cut by 33 to 50 percent. With better retention rates, too.

With all due respect to everyone quoted here, such claims must be met with a healthy dose of skepticism—or at least reservation. To simply state that e-learning *will* save you time, *will* save you money, and *will* provide a more capable workforce seems slightly authoritarian. Again, with the exception of Hall's benchmarking study, where's the proof? Read on.

In addition to saving gobs of money, online learning also saves tons of time, according to most industry consultants and vendors. Again, the elimination of travel is a big factor—but only one of many. The idea that employees can get up to half of their training at their PCs, precisely when they need it, is compelling.

Anytime training, or learn-as-you-go training, is a huge time saver for Charles Schwab and Co., according to Curtis Twombly, senior manager of Technology for Retail Client Services Training. "There used to be a time when you could pull everybody off the phones and put them in a classroom for a day. . . . [But] with increased business demands, classroom training no longer works."

> E-learning is saving 33 to 50 percent from the cost of training *while* cutting 50 percent off the time invested and allowing *better* results.

Why the emphasis on training costs/time? Because like it or not, training will continue to be *the* most important factor in terms of leveraging talent-in-place. According to published reports, surveys, and interviews, organizations all over the world are chiming in with the same numbers.

PricewaterhouseCoopers, the international accounting and business consulting giant. Prior to Price-Waterhouse's merger with Coopers, the company created a multimedia program called "Terminal RISK" to train its professional audit staff. Terminal RISK is a prerequisite for further training, and more than seven thousand people in fifty countries have taken advantage of it. To evaluate the effectiveness of the program, Price-Waterhouse conducted a training effectiveness review. Here are the findings, as compared to traditional classroom training:

- Terminal RISK reduced the time needed for learners to attain the same level of knowledge by 50 percent.
- The cost per learner for the technology-based training was $106 as opposed to $760 per learner (a savings of 87 percent).

The Rouse Company, of Columbia, Maryland, one of the largest real estate development and management companies in the United States, needed to train between six hundred and seven hundred employees in seventy different locations across the country. Like IBM, it worked with Lotus to develop a customized software solution using Lotus Learning Space. Results?

- The company cut training time by 68 percent without technical difficulties.
- It realized "an enormous return on investment" by eliminating travel costs.
- It achieved a high degree of employee satisfaction (4.3 on a scale of 5).

Intel Corporation is the world leader in microprocessors for the PC. The Logistics Systems training group previously offered traditional classroom instruction to the eight hundred employees for learning new applications. The training group incorporated embedded, technology-based training in the applications themselves, thus eliminating the need for classroom-led training.

- In one comparison of training time saved, the group determined that embedded e-learning cut the work time-missed for training by 83 percent (two hours missed from work, as opposed to twelve). As Brandon Hall points out, a ten-hour savings multiplied by eight hundred employees amounts to "a lot of productivity recaptured."

E-learning proponents insist that it's not just about saving on travel costs: it's about keeping employees, customers, vendors—the entire enterprise—up to speed on the latest products and services. Classroom training, as Schwab, IBM, and other top organizations have learned, just isn't able to cope with today's accelerating demands.

When Heather was at Learn2, she worked with a leading financial service organization that was changing its computer system over the weekend. Her company designed, developed, and delivered an e-learning course to employees to assure that, come Monday morning, the systems change would be seamless. Although this appeared a pricey solution at the outset, it was quickly seen as invaluable to the organization's ability to stay up running and responsive to customers.

OK, but what about the costs of such technology? How does an organization realize the inherent time/money advantages of e-learning without going broke in the short term? Hall's benchmarking study of best practices indicates that the costs for e-learning vary widely and are difficult to track. One reason Hall gives is that e-learning tends to "ride the corporate IT infrastructure" and is often intertwined with conventional training activities.

Also, e-learning is still in its childhood, baseline standards are still evolving, and to date there are few common metrics for measuring its effectiveness. Most of the discussion revolves around cost savings as opposed to true return on investment (ROI)—two very different kettles of fish. E-learning, in the Internet-based sense, is barely six years old and is already a sprawling, octopus-like entity with tentacles reaching into—and becoming entwined with—nearly every organizational nook imaginable, including IT, HR, marketing, and more. (Yes, we recommended this very strategy in the preceding chapter, and it is still good advice; it just makes standard ROI nigh impossible.) Online learning is a tough critter to track and measure with any accuracy.

Because of e-learning's slippery nature, at least in terms of measurement, some customers are beginning to question the claims. Does e-learning *really* save time or money? Is the ROI *really* worthwhile? And just when is the break-even point? One year? Two?

Let's take a closer look at some of these tentacles and see whether this octopus swims or just floats around spewing ink and gobbling budgets.

Are All These Claims True?

One of the caveats about online learning is that it takes more time and money to develop than many people expect. Major costs often are associated with Web-based training start-up. Once that hump is passed, though, the programs can be reused and modified repeatedly, thus costing much less than traditional classroom instruction.

Samantha Chapnick, CEO of Research Dog, isn't so sanguine. In a column for ASTD's *Learning Circuits* online magazine, she openly challenged these assertions, stating, "There are few claims as outlandish and unsubstantiated as e-learning being a money saver." She argues that the costs involved with traditional training (travel, lodging, instructors, material, etc.) are miniscule compared to the costs of e-learning.

"Just from the equipment perspective, you'll need multimedia computers with fast processors, modems or Ethernet cards and sound/video cards (at least $1,000 apiece), and a T1 line ($10,000/month). Hmm . . . seems more expensive than a few days in a hotel."[4]

While most organizations don't provide T1 or T3 lines for their employees, they do provide some kind of dial-up or modem connection. And they do purchase and maintain computers and networking infrastructure (LAN, WAN, etc.), all of which costs money. Suffice to say, a considerable outlay is involved—and this is only for the basic equipment. We're not even talking content, design, or LMSs yet.

As Chapnick indicates, the argument that usually follows is "But once you've made the initial investment, you'll never need to make it again—and *then* you'll realize all the cost benefits!" To which Chapnick answers, "I guess the people who make that argument are not familiar with Sierra's Law."[5]

Similar to Moore's Law (which states that processor speed doubles every eighteen months), Sierra's Law states that as processors get faster and hard drives get bigger, software makers will always create programs that require faster processors and more hard drive space than you have. (To say nothing of memory: Windows has bloated from requiring only two megs of RAM in Windows 3.1 to thirty-two megs in Windows XP.)

In addition to the physical costs of equipment and connectivity, there are also service and administration expenses to consider. Service costs include IT support for the organization's Internet, intranet, and LAN maintenance and initial implementation. Administration costs are somewhat murkier and include many of the "hidden" costs often overlooked when rolling out an e-learning initiative: legal, executive management, interdepartmental meetings, and so on. Few if any of these costs arise from traditional classroom training.

With service, you must account for the IT department's time and expertise in setting up, running, troubleshooting, and maintaining the infrastructure, which can include not only the Internet/intranet and e-learning software but also a million-dollar LMS. E-learning enthusiasts often discount these costs as part of the bullet one must bite when rolling out the initiative, often consigning them to the "equipment and hardware" part of the balance sheet. But ongoing IT time and labor are something that last far longer than the initial outlay.

Online learning, whether hosted remotely or behind the firewall, requires the ongoing involvement of IT. Says Chapnick, "IT must maintain and upgrade the computers, the Internet connections, the servers, and the software—even if it is just a browser. As the e-learning application gets more complex, IT's assistance becomes more crucial. Who will hook up all those webcams, and add the plug-ins to the initial footprint?"[6]

Then there are the "hidden" costs—administrative, logistics, and planning. When toting up the balance sheet for online learning, many managers overlook the costs of legal consultations, executive meetings, interdepartmental consultations, installation, training, implementation, and so forth. Yet, lawyers will be involved in vendor contracts, copyright negotiations, and other corporate legalities; executive management will be involved in planning and implementation meetings; division and department heads will interface with IT, HR, and training. All of this takes time and resources. So, where are the savings?

To verify the time and money claims (and to play devil's advocate), we contacted six of the most prominent e-learning users in the world, those organizations that have realized some of the greatest time and money savings—including IBM, Cisco, Intel, PwC, Charles Schwab, and KPMG. We wanted to know three things: (1) whether the optimism of the early days still applied, (2) whether the claims of time and money savings still held, and (3) what new time/money data or other measurement had been done recently.

But wait a minute. What does this have to do with *the learner*? That's the thrust of our book, isn't it? Focus on the Learner? Cater to the Learner? What do time or money savings have to do with *the learner*? Isn't this just another bite of the ROI apple?

Not really, because in order for you to have a learner, you must have some form of learning in place, right? And in order to have the learning in place, you must first gain approval from upper management, correct? You must Achieve Buy-in, in other words (chapter 2). We've already given you that particular tree. Now we'll give you the apples.

Online Learning—Money

Rob Wilkins, e-learning consultant with Pricewaterhouse-Coopers (PwC), in Sydney, Australia, shared our questions as to any inherent time or money savings with online learning. His main question was "*When* will we know we have been successful?" In other words, when and where do we measure e-learning?

"When we deliver an e-learning program," says Wilkins, "we should be able to *identify at which point we will know we have been successful*" (our emphasis). Wilkins goes on to do just that: identify his metrics for measuring e-learning. "Has productivity improved? Can that person use the software better? Has the bottom line increased? Has the person's attitude changed?" Anyone familiar with Kirkpatrick's four levels of assessment from the previous chapter will recognize these questions as pertaining to, respectively, Levels 4, 3, 4, and 2.

Wilkins speaks from experience. He knows what a successful, enterprise-wide e-learning program looks like—and how much one costs. "I implemented a successful e-learning program that provided people with an enhanced, interactive, and accelerated orientation experience," he told us. "After three years, we achieved savings over the $1 million (Australian) mark, and people were working in their jobs two weeks earlier [than with traditional training]. However, the program did not stand on its own. It had a lot of other systems and procedures wrapped around it. It also took a great deal of analysis to recommend the e-learning approach."

Did you catch that? "Other systems and procedures wrapped around it." "A great deal of analysis" (involving legal, executive, department, and division heads, etc.). Here are those hidden costs we mentioned. How much they chipped away at that $1 million mark is anyone's guess. Again, no standardized, all-inclusive metrics were in use at the time.

According to Wilkins, "Yes, I believe you *can* save time and money with e-learning. I believe you can also do it with one-on-one consultation, classroom learning, and other forms of training. It all comes down to being able to measure what you have done effectively."

But there's the rub: when times get tough, organizations often cut training programs before any results can be measured. Why? Because they are seen only as costs, not investments. As a result, says Wilkins, "no one knows the true value of learning to an organization. Sure, they have a general feeling, but no hard data to show them. You can *tell* the managing director how valuable the training is, but if you cannot *prove* it . . . ."

Wilkins believes this is where e-learning providers can and should take the next step: to include evaluation as part of their offering. Some already do—notably Docent, Lotus, and a few others—but they are the exception.

But should we even bother with all these attempts to measure learning? Executive and management consultant Marcia Daszko (www.mdaszko.com) thinks not. "Learning cannot be measured," she states. "Focus on metrics and they become the *only* thing that counts, not the learning or the learner." She is not alone in this view.

While we agree with her—that corporations, especially, tend to obsess on tracking, benchmarking, and measuring everything—we do recommend you perform some Level 4 or at least Level 3 assessments to prove that the investment is worthwhile. But we advise discretion. Don't make measurement the be-all and end-all of your online learning. You will lose site of the learner *and* the learning.

Yet, IT consultant and writer John Berry stresses the need for measurement. In an article for ASTD's *Learning Circuits,* he states that more companies today are trying to use metrics to measure e-learning's impact on strategic business goals (Level 4 assessment).

"Many businesses are only beginning to witness the dramatic cost savings in transitioning from traditional training to e-learning," Berry writes. "They have started ambitious measurement programs to prove e-learning's positive impact on customer service, productivity, and sales."[7]

As Berry points out, metrics can deliver such proof, which is why the Gartner Group estimates that up to 30 percent of its e-learning clients use some form of metrics to chart the impact of e-learning on the company's performance. Gartner claims that the use of metrics to justify e-learning will expand as more companies use online learning to support high-priority business goals, rather than run training programs for training's sake.

"I think it's a valid question to ask . . . what is the good of e-learning," says Clark Aldrich, formerly Gartner's research director for e-learning. "Is it just cost reduction? No. But does this translate into metrics? I think the new uses of e-learning are exceedingly interesting, and metrics are only one way to validate [them]."[8]

A compelling example is KPMG Consulting's recent revenue increases in e-commerce and e-business consulting. KPMG's success is testimony to the idea that benchmarking e-learning's contribution to the bottom line makes (dollars and) sense. The company estimated it would have taken three years to train its twenty-two thousand employees purely through classroom training in its own facility. Using a mix of classroom and e-learning around a custom curriculum, KPMG Consulting invested about $3 million to train eight thousand employees on e-business fundamentals in just *twelve weeks*. Soon after, the entire workforce completed the program.

The Gartner Group estimated that KPMG booked $1 billion in e-business consulting revenue following its e-learning rollout. KPMG knows the impact has been profound, even if it hasn't defined e-learning's contribution to revenue growth with strategic measurements.

"That's way ahead of the curve," says Douglas Stefanko, director of e-learning at KPMG Consulting. "A lot of people are still sorting out how to do e-learning, quite honestly, let alone how to start measuring it."[9] Our point exactly.

One idea, in terms of measuring the translation of new behaviors to increased revenue, is to compare sales and revenue growth after traditional classroom training against sales and revenue growth after e-learning. For most, it's a two-pronged fork: any e-learning initiatives are too young for meaningful measurement, and there's little to judge them by, due to a lack of measurement in the old days of traditional training. "We didn't capture metrics in the past because there really wasn't an alternative to classroom training," says Stefanko.[10]

Many of KPMG's competitors find themselves in the same quandary. At PricewaterhouseCoopers (PwC), roughly half the company's training curriculum is now delivered through e-learning, but no one's really sure of the impact on Level 3 or 4 matrices. Cindy Minetti, a director in PwC's management consulting services, says the company is just now beginning to measure e-learning's impact—data that will arise from measurement methodologies the company established several years ago, to track classroom training.

"Fundamentally, we believe our consultants are able to give reasonable insights into their own changed behaviors (Level 3) and business impact result (Level 4)," says Elizabeth Williams, a senior manager in PwC's learning and professional development group. "We take the 'reasonable evidence' point of view, and are not looking for conclusive proof in all cases."[11] Although this approach may seem subjective on the surface, such anecdotal evidence is often convincing.

Like many e-learning enthusiasts we interviewed, PwC insists that proof in the form of hard data really isn't necessary to confirm the bottom line benefits of e-learning. The company believes that "reasonable evidence" of e-learning's impact can be had by surveying management about improvements in employee performance. For example, if revenue has grown in one line of business, managers might be asked how much of that growth is attributable to e-learning versus other influences, such as marketing programs.

Then there's the Park Avenue Bank, in Valdosta, Georgia. Until two years ago, training at the bank involved giving employees a diskette-based program that had to be checked out and shared (i.e., via the library model). It could take days or even weeks for an individual to complete just one course. The training schedule for the entire institution was perpetually in jeopardy, since the diskettes might not be available when needed. Thus, training at the bank was a slow process, even though mandated by bank policy. Today, an Internet library of ninety-four courses has replaced the diskettes, offering training in a host of subjects (regulations, security, compliance, teller skills, etc.)

"In this fast-paced world in which we live, anything that saves time, saves money," says Emily Anderson, the bank's program director for marketing and training. "Since going online, our employees are taking courses at their convenience 24 hours a day, 7 days a week. That's real-time in today's world."[12]

Since most employees at all five bank locations have access to the Internet, they no longer have to search for a laptop and the right training diskette. They simply enter their user ID and password to access the library at a convenient time—before work, during lunch, after work, or at home—from any computer that offers Internet access.

So far, employees at the $244 million bank have completed over seven hundred online courses, and Anderson is hooked on e-learning. She promoted the online concept to her management team as a way to ensure employees got the training they needed in a manner that was most convenient for them.

SmartForce recently helped a prominent American consulting firm measure the sales impact of an e-learning curriculum on e-business nine months after the training period ended. The firm had no prior e-business revenue whatsoever. "We went to the partner and asked, 'What part of this do you think you would attribute to the training?'" according to Christine Pope, director of consulting services. "The company won $10 million in e-business consulting, $1 million of which management was prepared to hang on the e-learning investment. The e-learning cost was roughly $200,000."[13]

That's some ROI.

But remember what Jay Cross said about ROI: it ain't what it used to be. The old yardsticks no longer apply, and they can actually get in the way. As Cross posits, "Why measure incremental improvements when you're seeking the Holy Grail?"

True, traditional financial analysis works in most business accounting, but it goes askew when measuring intellectual capital and other off-the-balance-sheet improvements. Making business decisions entails a wide range of factors and involves intricate trade-offs—it's not all bottom-line dollars and cents.

Says Cross, "Unless your training (or e-learning) unit sells training for a fee—generating its own revenues—the returns on investment come from satisfying the needs of business unit managers." He advises that linking e-learning results to business results is more useful than coming up with pseudo-ROI figures. "The only valid training ROI is business ROI."[14]

International Data Corporation (IDC) studied the buying behavior of corporate and IT training managers and concluded that ROI will no longer be measured in savings or reduced cost of training. Instead, attention will be directed to "measurable changes to business metrics resulting from training investments." Those benefits will only emerge, however, if vendors focus on solid instructional design and engaging learning environments.

Thus, a senior manager's appraisal of e-learning's impact is often visceral (gut instinct), based on how satisfied he or she is with employee performance and how much of that improvement the manager can ascribe to e-learning. As Cross puts it, "Feelings win out because the assumptions used to create the (ROI) numbers can always be challenged. Projects that evoke the *best feelings* make the cut."[15]

Why? Because managers own the problems that training solves—online or offline. They're generally pragmatic, and their overriding interest is to get the job done now, if not sooner. The business unit manager is often e-learning's primary sponsor—along with HR and IT. Moreover, the manager understands the goal of *any* training, since it is he or she who oversees the environment in which performance gaps occur. Thus, the first step in measuring e-learning's impact on performance is eliciting the business manager's answer to the classic query "What's in it for me?"

Remember our description in chapter 1 of the front-end alignment and how we determine an organization's business objectives? We actually get senior-level executives and unit managers to *verbalize their goals* (and, in so doing, learn what's in it for them). Once everyone agrees on the goals, we examine *each job* in light of these aims—to see what each *should* contribute toward accomplishing those goals. After that, we isolate the most accomplished performers at each job, model (or "paradigm") their behavior, then construct modules, lessons, courses, and job aids based on those paradigms—logical, clockwork accomplishmentment-based curriculum design.

Same with metrics and tracking e-learning. First, gain agreement on the problem and the value of solving it. Then outline how you propose to solve it. Establish a benchmark of current performance, and clearly indicate how performance will be tracked and reported.

Some insist it's impossible to isolate the impact of e-learning—or any training, for that matter. You can never tell whether some other influence (e.g., marketing or competitor miscues) may have affected the results, thus negating their value as evidence of e-learning's impact.

Mark Turner, of GPe, describes how his organization partners with clients long before any e-learning takes place, in order to define benchmarks to be measured against later. "The process of tracking e-learning's impact begins way before any learning takes place," he says. "It starts by partnering with the business unit manager who owns the problem. We then determine what skill or knowledge gaps exist in the workforce, and it's upon that data that we construct not only our learning architecture but also any benchmarking for later analysis."

In most cases, Turner says, he gathers information through interviews that focus on the work process, not training. These interviews should always bear in mind the mother of all training questions: "What difference would this make?" A joint examination of the problem will pinpoint the gap between the results the manager wants and the results he or she will actually get. Then, Turner's group determines what major skill gaps and learning deficiencies might be holding people back.

When the learning is completed, assess the results according to benchmark measurements established with the unit manager. "Extrapolate behavior changes into measurable business," counsels Jay Cross. "There's no room for vagueness—and no backing away from visible quantitative evidence." He also suggests that further interviewing and a review of business results may be useful.

Finally, Cross advises presenting any findings and a simple cost/benefit analysis to the business manager or training sponsor—not a full-blown "ROI."

As Cross and others point out, present-day accounting is an anachronism when applied to e-learning. "Traditional accounting only recognizes physical entities," Cross explains. "Intangibles are valued at zero. Vast areas of human productivity—ideas, abilities, experience, insight, esprit de corps, motivation—lie outside its vision field. It doesn't recognize that people become more valuable over time."

To many corporate executives today—Cross included—the traditional concept of training ROI is obsolete. Business unit managers value time more than ROI. Major decisions are based on descriptive business cases, not pro forma budgets. Senior executives tend to be more interested in the top line (dynamic growth from new markets and innovation) than the bottom line (the accounting fiction of profits). Why? The answer, according to Cross, is simple:

"The 'Net changes everything."

Online Learning—Time

Now that we have examined the claims about online learning's built-in money savings, let's look at the much-ballyhooed time savings. Although we have touched on this second benefit already, we felt it worthy of a more in-depth examination here.

Few things move faster than a jet (except office gossip), so we zoomed into a review of online learning at the Federal Aviation Administration (FAA). Everyone involved in the airline industry—pilots, air traffic controllers, maintenance personnel, airport security, designers, technicians, programmers, environmental specialists—gets their required training and certification through the FAA—specifically, through the FAA Academy, the agency's training facility in Oklahoma City.

Established in 1959, the academy for decades relied solely on traditional classroom training, bringing in vast numbers of students from around the country to its Oklahoma City resident training facilities. Due to the detailed nature of the training, many students had to leave their families and jobs for extended periods, often weeks or months at a time.

To compound matters, as a federal agency the FAA Academy increasingly found itself embroiled in budget battles. Continued demands to reduce FAA budgets, coupled with the massive travel, lodging, and lost productivity expenses of resident training, led the agency to pursue alternatives to the classroom. These led to the creation of a distributed learning solution called the Interactive Video Teletraining (IVT) network, an elegant blend of distributed *and* online learning.

Broadcasting from a presentation server, an instructor can reach students anywhere in the world. They see and hear the instructor on a classroom TV and interact by pressing a button on the response keypad. By using the "call" key, students engage the instructor in conversation, while everyone on the network can hear questions and responses.

The FAA was one of the first federal agencies to adopt interactive video teletraining. While the benefits have been dramatic, convincing Congress to approve the shift to IVT was not easy. Rich Schrum, the FAA's IVT operations manager, says, "We had to prove to Congress not only that our proposed IVT network was cost-effective but that the training was as good as our established resident training system."

In terms of pure time savings, the academy realized startling results with its Dangerous Goods and Cargo Security Program. Over four days, the academy trained several hundred security personnel using thirty-seven receiver sites. Says Schrum, "Courses that would have required between eight and sixteen hours to conduct in Oklahoma City were completed remotely in six hours, due to the efficiency of the multimedia-based presentation." The only people who had to travel were three subject-matter experts who flew to the academy to present the information.

"The program's manager contacted me afterward to tell me how pleased she was," Schrum adds. "She calculated the entire four-day program was delivered to 318 students at a cost to the taxpayers of only $18 per student. As anyone in training can tell you, that's pretty good."[16]

There's the time savings—and significant cost savings as well.

Cisco's online training times have improved 66 percent in the last year alone. Whereas it formerly took three months to get an employee up to speed in a manufacturing facility, with Cisco's new approach that time is down to just four weeks.

OK, so everyone's saving time and money with e-learning; the claims are proving to be more fact than myth. But what was that we heard about *making money*? Can you actually *make money* with online training?

Online Learning *Makes* Money?

Yep. Our studies have found that not only does online learning save time and money, but it can also *make* money for certain users. How? The answer involves another "e-": e-commerce. Using e-learning on e-commerce Web sites to educate shoppers and cross-sell products is a boon.

Future.com predicts that 42 percent of e-learning will be used to educate the customer or consumer about a product.[17]

Advertising and e-commerce represent an enormous opportunity for e-learning applications. They are perfect examples of the importance of partnerships between traditional institutions and for-profit providers. And their potential value directly hinges on how tightly integrated e-learning providers become with educational, commercial, and other intranets.

For example, we recently browsed a Web site touting various crockery and cookware items. As a companion piece, the Web site also offered a list of natural herbal recipes, which incorporated not only the herbs and spices in one's garden but also—you guessed it—the cookware the company was selling. It turns out many (if not all) of the recipes worked ever so much better with the company's cookware.

This is but one example. You'll see it with financial services firms, automotive companies—even the fabulous LL Bean invested millions of dollars to educate its buyers to make more informed (and hopefully more frequent) buying decisions. As Internet-savvy companies large and small gain a bigger share of the increasing numbers of online shoppers, there are literally billions of dollars to be made. Extra dollars—above and beyond what the company would have made without "webucating" its Web site visitors. Even schools and universities are taking note and cranking up.

As mentioned in our introduction, many schools today offer online learning. Yet they must compete with the big-name service providers for Internet space. One way to attract—and keep—students is to entertain and cross-sell to them (e.g., get your credit hours in anthropology and the course text, *Anthropology Today*, here for a limited time only!). Schools can now provide students with goods and services they *need* while capturing some of the revenue that would have gone to another vendor.

HOW TO CAPITALIZE ON E-LEARNING

So, you're not Ernst and Young, Cisco, or IBM. You're Do-Dah Heating and Air, and you want a scalable, customized e-learning solution for your technicians—something you can get up and running with a minimum of fuss and realize a maximum of knowledge, skills, and training for your people. You don't have a whopping budget. You may only have one desktop computer or two. You don't know a "hub" from a hubcap and couldn't really care less. What to do?

Look to the learner. What are the real needs? What are the options available?

As Jay Cross points out, investment analysts seem to think that harvesting the rewards of e-learning is a breeze. "Simply convert your existing content to digital form, slap it onto the corporate intranet, and immediately save millions in travel, bricks and mortar, and instructor salaries while training all those IT workers everyone needs."[18] Alas, such is not the case. You've got to customize the learning for the learners.

Yet, the costs of creating customized content, infrastructure, an LMS, and so forth, is prohibitive for many midsize to smaller businesses. What then? Order up a library of generic, off-the-shelf content and slap it on an intranet? No, no, and again, *no*.

Increasingly, the answer today is to *use an e-learning portal*. Workplace Web portals can vary widely, offering everything from standard company fare to advanced streaming multimedia. A survey of HR professionals from 350 companies released in 1999 by the Hunter Group found that technology companies are early adopters of employee portals, with 71 percent of such companies reporting that they have a strategy in place. But they are ahead of the time.

Six in ten companies surveyed by the Hunter Group said they don't have an e-learning portal strategy in place.

The second part of this strategy is to *start small*. One of the most attractive and powerful advantages of e-learning is its scalability. You don't have to start with the whole pie, the LMS, the knowledge management, the complete infrastructure, and so forth. The trick is to start small and keep it simple. Many programs are already available that you can promote for your employees, rather than reinvent the wheel.

Ask a handful of employees to take a course, then get their feedback. Listen to the providers as well, but remember that claims aren't evidence. Find your own references, because nobody gives out bad ones.

We also caution smaller to midsize businesses that no single learning experience or delivery method is ideal for everyone. Online learning is not a one-size-fits-all solution. Also, not every employee will be motivated enough to benefit from purely online training. The magic is in the mix—a strategic combination of classroom and e-learning delivery.

The possibilities are limited only by your imagination.

What Works

- Understand your true investment.
- Start small and scale upward.
- It takes time and money to save time and money.
- Be sure it really does save dollars and time and, most of all, makes sense.

4 | Tame the Technology

I think there is a world market for maybe five computers.
　　　　　　　—Tom Watson, IBM chairman, 1943

Who the hell wants to hear actors talk?
　　　　　　　—H. M. Warner, Warner Brothers, 1927

While modern technology has given people powerful new communication tools, it apparently can do nothing to alter the fact that many people have nothing useful to say.
　　　　　　　—Leo Gomes

CASE STUDY ▪ Buckman Laboratories

Buckman Laboratories, a $300 million chemical company with 1,300 people in seventy countries, makes over five hundred products in eight factories around the world. Its main product, however, is knowledge—about its clients, products, vendors, and people.

Owner Bob Buckman's challenge was to close the gap with customers by sharing corporate brainpower worldwide. He asked, "How do we stay connected? How do we share knowledge? How do we function anytime, anywhere?" The knowledge stream had to be easily accessible, rapidly shared, and useful to clients. Buckman partnered with CompuServe, launching his own online learning site (K'Netix) for leveraging the corporation's global brainpower.[1]

The only problem was getting people to use it.
"We had to turn the company's culture upside down," says Buckman. And, with the captain firmly on deck, that's precisely what happened: a complete corporate turnaround, steered by Buckman and propelled by incentives. For example, Buckman organized a celebration at a Scottsdale, Arizona, resort to recognize the company's 150 best knowledge sharers. Winners received a new IBM ThinkPad 755, a leather computer bag, and a mind-opening presentation by Tom Peters.

Here are the keys Bob Buckman used to unlock the company's global potential and open the gates to twenty-first-century knowledge technologies:

- Reduce "technostress." Rather than ordering everyone to use the system at work, Buckman encouraged employees to test the waters in a relaxed atmosphere (i.e., from home, on breaks, etc.).
- Make it fun. At Buckman, this meant contests, prizes, and plenty of PR.
- Nominate experts. System operators (SysOps) appointed two experts in each forum as primary answer givers. These are subject-matter experts (SMEs) whom anyone anywhere can access for answers.
- Include everyone. Buckman's dictum is "You never know where the answer will come from." So why not include everyone? This minimizes the risk of untapped potential.
- Make it easy. User-friendliness is a given. On K'Netix, the icons are simple and the access is easy: just point and click.[2]

UNDERSTAND THE TECHNOLOGY (IT'S NOT THAT TOUGH)

Sing along with us now to the alphabet song, "AOL, B2C, HTML, MP3. . . ." Acronyms, buzzwords, and jargon, oh my! Just listen to the *sound* of technology. Can't we call it a "picture" or a "graphic" instead of a gif, a jpg, or a bmp? How many bits, bytes, RAMs, and gigapoogles ya got? Technical folks, please be kind to the learners. And, learners, it's time to wake up and smell the keyboard.

Some people just don't get it. The technologies invading their jobs, homes, and places of recreation simply boggle them. Many working professionals today are loathe to admit it, but the truth is, the technology scares them.

News flash: online learning isn't that tough. The technology, the infrastructure—even Learning Management Systems—aren't that hard to grasp, once someone shows you the tools. One of the toughest thing about it all is the jargon; like the law or the priesthood, e-learning is shrouded in cryptospeak, high folderol, and ever-changing buzzwords—the better to hold the masses in awe and keep authority in the hands of a chosen few. Once you do your homework, it's not that hard to understand—or nearly as frightening as you thought it would be. Call it an e-piphany.

After all, everything we do today involves technology. Everything's digital. We do practically nothing the way our parents did. Everything we do involves bytes, bits, and microchips. Why should learning be any different? Like other forms of communication, online learning simply avails itself of the latest technologies in place.

Yet, many managers and executives just don't get it. They're still struggling with all the other technological advancements that have invaded their lives. They feel uncomfortable because they can no longer flip a record onto the turntable and play it but must instead program a DVD player. (The DVD, incidentally, replaced a CD that replaced a cassette that replaced their old vinyl record years ago.) They're depressed that they no longer "cook" their food but must instead program a microwave oven to nuke it. The VCR they bought (which they never could program in the first place) is now outmoded by TiVO (which they cannot program, either). As for computers? Networks? Routers, hubs, and ethernets? Forget about it.

It's called *technophobia:* that horrible mixture of fear, embarrassment, and frustration many of us experience when forced to operate some piece of high-tech gadgetry—

anything from a programmable cell phone to the latest, greatest Pentium V 2.8GHz multimedia superputer. This fear and resentment is understandable; for many, the technology has come out of nowhere and been foisted upon them without the slightest warning. Yet, it is a major obstacle for any organization trying to embrace online learning. Our prescriptive list of ingredients for taming the technology is as follows:

Studies by a number of researchers indicate that most of us are uncomfortable, to varying degrees, with technology.[3]

- Understand what technophobia is and how to reduce it.
- Appreciate the cultural/organizational causes or influences.
- Commit to organization-wide technological training.
- Model best practices, and practice what you preach.
- Link technological expertise to career advancement.
- Offer rewards/incentives for increased technological skills.
- Provide ongoing support and mentoring.

Ideally, online learning fits into the equation everywhere. Every day and in every way. The technology must not get in the way. E-learning should be *one with the job process:* a fluid, seamless symbiosis of learning, doing, and knowing. And the technology should be so intuitive, so subtle, it virtually disappears.

Computer, networking, and Internet technologies have become so powerful, varied, and pervasive, even the techno-savvy sometimes run into a (fire)wall. Thousands of companies today employ whole staffs just to run their networks.

Meanwhile, in their prairie dog cubicles, employees by the millions are milling about their work stations, puttering at their Macs, or riding herd on their PCs, hoping against hope not to see the dreaded Blue Screen of Death. Which, more often than not, they do. IT staffs today spend most of their time putting out fires and explaining the inexplicable. So where does e-learning fit into all this? Answer: *Everywhere.*

Truly human-friendly technological design won't appear anytime soon. Computer, networking, and software engineers cast the die five decades ago, and nothing short of a technological revolution will alter the standard model. We simply have to use what we have in the simplest, most streamlined ways possible. Otherwise, technophobia could be the killer that nails your app to the wall. The technology that made e-learning possible could be the very thing that murders it.

And there's the rub, according to Donald Norman, president of UNext learning systems and renowned author on technology and its effect on people. Norman believes the reason for all this technostress has nothing to do with us. It's the people who design the technology.

A study in *USA Today* showed that the average computer user waits ten seconds for a Web page to load before clicking to the next page.

"The best way to cure technophobia is to cure the reasons that cause it; that is, to design things that people can use," Norman says, in his CD-ROM called *Defending Human Attributes in the Age of the Machine*.[4] He is also author of the books *The Design of Everyday Things* and *Things That Make Us Smart*.

Norman is the voice of one crying in the wilderness of technophobia. Although his focus is on all things technological, much of what he says and writes applies to e-learning—especially the e-learner.

Similarly, Michelle Weil and Larry Rosen, clinical psychologists based in California, have done extensive research over the past fifteen years exploring the effect of technology on humans. They define three distinct technology attitude groups:

1. **Eager Adopters** (10 to 15 percent of the population): These are the geeks, dweebs, and nerds who *love* technology. They lust after the latest gadgetry: cell phones, big-screen TVs, DVD players, and computers. They love tinkering with the newest and most modern technologies available and

will spend hours experimenting with them. (Hackers are a neurotic subspecies of this group.)

2. **Hesitant Prove-its** (50 to 60 percent): These are the Missourians among us—the "Show me" folks. Although the Hesitant Prove-its don't actively resist technology, they need to be shown how it can improve their lives—enhance their work and play, not interfere with it. (John straddles the first two groups.)

3. **Resistors** (30 to 40 percent): These are the true technophobes, the ones who are all thumbs with high-tech goodies and who actively feel threatened, embarrassed, or intimidated by it. They are the modern-day Luddites in our midst. (Heather *was* here but is now clicking her way up the technoladder.)

So, out of the box most of your learners will resist the "e-" before they even get to the learning.

Studies by Weil, Rosen, and others say that these percentages mean that 85 to 90 percent of an organization's employees may be technophobic to some degree and uncomfortable with new technology.[5]

According to Weil and Rosen, "This wouldn't be so bad if we could opt out, but people don't have much of a choice anymore. . . . Technology isn't going away."

Why bother addressing technophobia? Isn't it a matter of "like it or lump it"? The idea that employees should have help with new technologies is admittedly not a popular one with most directors and managers. Such help entails costs, time, and loss of productivity. Besides, shouldn't employees already have basic computer and networking skills? During the 1980s and '90s, the attitude in corporate America was that employees would simply either sink or swim—with a lifeline tossed out occasionally from IT. For many organizations, this was the only practical answer.

But was it ever really practical? What happens in the workplace when such an attitude prevails? As Dennis Hopper used to say in the Nike commercials, "Bad things, man. Ba-a-a-d things."

A few examples come to mind:

- Employees unfamiliar with the new technology will not be committed to using it
- Uncommitted employees over time may become unmotivated, belligerent, and hostile
- Even dedicated employees can disrupt or damage office systems if not conversant with the technology (enthusiasm + incompetence = disaster).
- Employees may revert to prior methods of doing things if new technology isn't properly introduced

Robert Heverly, writing for the Capitol District Business Review's *In-Depth: Office Quarterly,* says that administrators introducing new technologies into the workplace should be conversant with the systems they're implementing. To simply foist new technology onto employees and hope for the best is like whistling past the graveyard. (Quick question: How many of you know, or perhaps *are,* someone who prints out e-mails, hand-writes—maybe dictates—the reply, then has someone else type it back and send it for you?)

"The people in charge of administrating any new technology or system should be completely trained in its use and implementation,"[6] Heverly states. In other words, if your office is moving from a Windows 95–based local area network (LAN) to a Windows NT LAN, the administrator should be taught the basics of WinNT networking, how the computers are connected, how the network software and hardware operates, and so on.

All fine and good. But what about the employees? The customers? The *learners*? Remember strategy 1: Cater to the Learner. As Heverly points out, training for employees is the most basic element; it should be provided by a professional trainer skilled in using the technology in question. Better still, the training *itself* should be embedded in the e-learning software. Ditto measurement. And tracking.

We're about to embark on a concise examination of the technologies currently in place for e-learning. This is by no means an all-inclusive survey, as many new technologies, or new twists on current ones, will hit the market before this book does. But in the main, most of what we'll analyze here will still apply by the time you read this. The following is intended not only for the HR or IT professional struggling to get an e-learning initiative off the ground but also for the *provider who seeks entry into the market.*

ARE YOU MANAGING THE SYSTEM OR IS IT MANAGING YOU?

When a chessmaster sits down to examine a chess position, whether in the opening stage or the end game, he or she often ponders, "If only I could. . . ." Meaning, "If only I could arrange the pieces into *this* position or *that* position, then I could have this (or that) outcome."

Similarly, when examining your online learning position, always bear in mind the desired result for the learner: if not checkmate, then surely a mating (or meeting) of technology, learning, knowing, and doing on the job—a state of *learnativity*, as Marcia Conner and Wayne Hodgins describe it (see www.learnativity.com).

First, make sure your organization has the hardware necessary to support the software, networking, and e-learning programs involved. This sounds like a no-brainer, but we never cease to be amazed by the number of organizations struggling to implement multimedia e-learning programs whose PCs lack compatible sound cards or speakers.

Employee hardware, technical skills, readiness, attitude, and so forth, all must be in place *before* serving up your e-learning. The big consideration here? WIIFM: *What's in it for me?* Smart CLOs and CIOs will *connect technological readiness with career advancement* in the employee's mind, early and often.

Important: For e-learners with disabilities, be sure to provide assistive technology as needed to enhance access, such as touch-sensitive screens, head-mounted pointers, word prediction software, and voice input technology. For further information, write to Office of Special Education and Rehabilitative Services, U.S. Department of Education, Mary E. Switzer Building, 330 C Street S.W., Washington, D.C. 20202; or phone (202) 205-5465.

So much for the basic hardware. What about the infra-structure? What about the different types of e-learning de-livery? Application service providers? Internet, intranet, and extranet? And what about those Web site learning portals? Relax. As we stated at the outset of this chapter, don't be overwhelmed by the dizzying array of technologies and technobabble floating around. It all boils down to one thing: using the Internet to store and deliver learning to the desktop.

Most—if not all—of your basic infrastructure is probably already in place. If you manage in today's workplace, you manage a network. You no doubt already have at least a jostling acquaintance with your intranet (the company's own, in-house version of the Internet). You may even have some familiarity with the company Web site or plans for one. If so, you're already on your way. The only decision now is whether to create your e-learning in-house, with your own, customized content, running on your own intranet, or to outsource as much as possible and rely on a ASP or other "hosted" service or learning portal. The choice is yours.

Certainly, outsourcing to a technology partner is least expensive in the short term. Such a partner's staff handles the e-learning software, infrastructure, content, tracking, and evaluation (if any). They wrestle with all the IT headaches, networking issues, and other matters. But while you may save on initial outlay, you may lose on customiza-tion and control—to say nothing of immediate updates.

The other solution is to partner early on with your own IT department, presenting the staff there with your e-learning problem, goals, and budget constraints. The potential is far greater control of the program, more extensive customiza-tion, and more responsiveness to your management and training needs.

Partner with IT early and often. This is the advice of Tom Kelly, VP of e-learning solutions for Cisco. In a recent inter-view, Kelly outlined for us a profound yet simple road map for e-learning that Cisco uses. Kelly calls it the

Three Key Success Factors—Ten Lessons Learned

- **First key success factor:** Partner early and com-pletely with your IT department. Organizations usually try to push e-learning in HR or training, but not IT. But you must partner with IT from the start. And don't tell the IT staff what training outcomes you want. Instead, bring them a business problem, not a solution. Let them determine the road to the solution.

- **Second key success factor:** Focus on *business issues*, not training problems. Any metrics to success have to be built around business issues—customer satisfaction foremost.

- **Third key success factor:** Don't think of e-learning as "just" training but learning, education, communication, *and* training. Like e-mail, e-learning is basically a form of communication.

Ten Lessons Learned, in Reverse Order

10. **You must have executive *stakeholders*, not merely executive *support*.** Support evaporates once an initiative becomes difficult and it's relegated to Mission Impossible.

9. **Use virtual project teams.** Bring experts in, make your online movie *once*, then send them back to their real jobs. Engineers don't like being away from their work.

8. **Chart visible career paths.** Cisco calls it "snare and share": get the technical info and send it out. People will use it.

7. **Regard certification as the goal.** Measure everything. You have no clue what the correlation of impacts are going to be down the road.

6. ***Be the learner* when creating content.** Focus on learner-centric design. Find out what learners need, how, and then create it—don't base content or delivery solely on technology or trainers. To quote Tom Kelly, "Putting training people in charge of e-learning is like putting postal workers in charge of e-mail."

5. **Remember that marketing is your friend.** If you build it (i.e., e-learning), chances are nobody will care unless you make a splash. You must have a formal marketing/communications plan about what you're doing, why, and what impact it has on the company and the learner.

4. **Remember that IT is your *best* friend.** "Content is king, but infrastructure is God," Kelly says. Without infrastructure, you can't be successful; and without infrastructure partnership, you're DOA.

3. **Innovate and standardize.** Focus on a standard set of tools and Big Rules, not petty details. Get IT support around that standardization. You still have to innovate, keep your standards evolving, to keep up with new tools and technologies that work for you.

2. **You're now a dot.com, so you'll have to change your funding mind-set.** Most training groups have an internal charge-back system in which they pay $250 to $300 a day for people to attend traditional training. That's fair. But how do you charge for six minutes of video?

1. **Celebrate team successes, and learn how to partner.** Create a vendor database. Explore vendors and seek out experts and organizations in *different areas of training expertise.*

By following these guidelines, Tom Kelly and the Cisco e-learning team have helped their organization cut training times for employees by more than 66 percent.

CREATING TRAINING THAT PEOPLE CAN USE

When creating training that people *can* use, remember to provide access to an expert in the technology—someone who is available, by phone, in the office, or by instant messaging, to assist employees in migrating to the technology. Usually, this is someone in your own IT department—"the computer guy/gal" who flickers into offices and remedies computer problems like a digital age Florence Nightingale, then shimmers away again to help some other cyber-challenged employee. There aren't enough of these people to go around, however, as the IT gap in the United States is still growing.

Also, access to subject-matter experts (SMEs) or content experts is also necessary—not merely desirable. E-learners stuck in a lesson might not want to interrupt a live, synchronous online classroom session. Self-paced learners similarly stuck might not be able to find any answers online. Yet, access to SMEs is crucial—so crucial, in fact, that several e-learning providers include expert access in their product offering.

Says Paul Earl, CEO of Interactive Training, Inc., "Our courseware provides an onscreen 'Expert Link,' which the learner can click to have instant access to the expert behind the content. We feel this kind of rapid feedback is essential to the success of both the learner and our e-learning offering."

Furthermore, if employees feel as if they are on their own after the training, technophobia may reappear, with employees returning to prior methods of accomplishing tasks. This not only mitigates any training received but also frustrates the usefulness of the technology, the worker(s) involved, and the administration.

Another strategy we highly recommend when introducing or changing technology in the workplace is allowing the affected employees to *play with* and *learn* about it. A great example of this is the introduction of the Internet and the World Wide Web into the work environment. If you want employees to be able to use the Web to find data or do research, let them surf the Web freely before asking them to perform specific functions in relation to it.

True, this could mean allowing employees to visit entertainment Web sites, Internet shopping catalogs, or other non-job-related sites on company time, but what of it? Think of the weeks of time employees waste each year in compulsory, boring, and unproductive meetings. Any "play-and-learn" will be worth it in the long run and shouldn't impinge on productivity to any great extent. Time limits can be set by managers at the outset and presented to the learners ahead of time.

Such interaction with new technology in a mainly stress-free environment allows the employee to learn about that technology and grow into it. Thus, when a work-related task does come along, the employee can complete it more quickly and efficiently using the new technology to its fullest and, in doing so, learn still more.

One final element of a successful technostrategy is to *commit the entire office* to the new technology. Nothing frustrates employees struggling with new technology more than seeing senior office staff or administrators gleefully still using the old technology while they must learn and implement the new one. Insisting that all levels adopt and use the new technology is a solid way to ensure that employees take seriously the firm's commitment to the new technology and implement it accordingly.

How do we help learners learn how to e-learn? First, remember that everything hinges on the learner. Second, remember the domino theory from chapter 1: we set up our dominoes in each step and find them falling into place in successive steps. Now, when it comes to using the technology to teach users how to use that technology, you'll be relieved to find your dominoes are already in place. When you perform your first gap analysis and needs assessment, be sure to include a technological assessment of each learner. Which brings us to step 1:

1. Assess the learners' skills and attitudes toward technology. Divide them into learning groups based on current skill levels, if possible.
2. Have an expert in both technology and learner-focused training teach the new technology without jargon.

3. Ensure technology instruction is hands-on for all users. Use graduated simulation exercises in a low-risk setting so learners can experiment.

4. Chunk the learning. Limit instruction time to what the new user can assimilate and retain (i.e., no more than thirty minutes per module).

5. Practice what you preach. Managers and higher-ups should know and use the technology every day.

6. Use the same hardware and software for training as learners will use on the job.

7. Create and maintain easy access to an expert user after training.

8. Employers need to *value* technology and connect learner proficiency to career advancement. Otherwise, what's in it for me?[7]

It's important to ensure that any new technology will be successfully integrated into every part of the organization. According to Weil and Rosen, if employers don't understand there are technophobes in the company who may need additional help, then they will suffer reduced worker productivity and profits, decreased efficiency, and increased errors with higher employee absenteeism.

On the other hand, taking care to recognize and implement different training interventions for different worker attitudes and expertise levels better ensures desired outcomes: improved productivity, cost savings, and job satisfaction. By reducing workplace technophobia, you'll be well on your way to more effective technology implementation and use.

CREATING TRAINING THAT PEOPLE WILL USE

We've seen the kind of online learning that people *can* use. But what about the kind of online learning that people *will* use? What will attract potential learners and make them actual, successful learners? If we build it, will they come?

According to the latest numbers from Nua.com, the world's leading resource for Internet trends and usage, the number of Internet users worldwide is 513.41 million (as of August 2001). Of these, Canadian and American users account for 180.68 million users. See the following list:

Internet Users[8]

Area	Number (in millions)
Africa	4.15
Europe	154.63
Canada and United States	180.68
Asia/Pacific	143.99
Middle East	4.65
Latin America	25.33

A survey by FIND/SVP, a New York City research firm, found that twenty million Americans rely on the Internet daily. An additional 9.3 million Americans tried the 'Net during the preceding year but did *not* consider themselves users.[9]

"The Internet is presently a study in contrasts," said Thomas Miller, who directed the American Internet User Survey. "Regular users have become dependent on it, but nearly half of all users still rate the Internet somewhat to very difficult to use."

Even those who use the Internet daily have concerns about its ease of use—or lack thereof. A survey by MCI One found that 68 percent of the people who currently don't use communications technology (i.e., the Internet, pagers, and cellular phones) feel technophobic about those technologies.

A more recent study released in May 2001, by ASTD and the Masie Institute revealed three crucial success factors in determining whether an employee will accept and use a work-related e-learning course:

- **Internal marketing:** Be sure to promote your online learning well in advance, so employees are prepared.

- **Support:** Employees respond better to e-learning when they have technical, subject-matter, and managerial support.

- **Incentives:** Show employees the value of the learning—links to career advancement.

Mark Van Buren, director of research for ASTD, notes, "There is clear evidence that the context and manner in which e-learning is offered affects employee receptivity—regardless of the type of e-learning or the course design."

Elliott Masie, president of the Masie Center and coproducer of the study, adds, "While we know that it takes brochures, catalogs, and telephone calls to fill many classroom offerings, there is a dysfunctional tendency to underinvest in the marketing of online learning modules."[10]

One phase of the study looked at how sixteen companies (fifteen of which are among the Fortune 500) attract learners to mandatory and voluntary e-learning courses. This portion of the study revealed that learners are drawn to courses that *blend e-learning with other forms of instruction* and courses in which they can learn away from their busy desks.

The companies tracked learners' acceptance of Internet-, intranet-, and CD ROM–based online learning as part of twenty-nine carefully selected courses, aimed at audiences of seventy-one to six thousand employees. Most of the learners were sales or business professionals, and the e-learning content they received varied from product information to professional skills content. The findings indicated that it wasn't the learning technologies themselves that hampered or intimidated learners, it was the lack of an "overriding organizational imperative."[11]

> "The hardest part isn't the technology; it's the cultural issue of getting people used to the fact that it's part of their job."
>
> —KEVIN OAKES, chairman and CEO, Click2Learn

Doug Foster, vice president of services for Click2Learn, adds that the technology already exists to integrate learning into learners' jobs so they can take things in small chunks (just as much as they need, just when they need it). The issue is the corporate culture. "The learners have to know that they're expected to use it, they're expected to learn, and if they don't understand something, they should ask questions," Foster says.

He adds that employees expert in any area should share that knowledge with the organization, thus aiding what he terms a "reciprocal culture."

Understanding the Internet and related technologies is the door through which any e-learning provider must pass. Understanding how to use those technologies to deliver engaging, relevant, as-needed content is the key to unlocking that door. For, if your e-learning offering can be described by all three of those adjectives—*engaging, relevant,* and *as-needed*—you will have e-learning that people *will* use.

And understanding the need for a corporate/cultural turn-around that emphasizes the learner is the tumbler in that lock.

Even under ideal cultural conditions, in a learner-focused environment that emphasizes technical proficiency, the technology can still stymie even the most advanced users—not because of a lack of anything but because of a surfeit. The amazing array of available choices in learning, designing, tracking, and such, is mind-boggling. The technology is so flexible, users and designers will always have several ways of achieving the same learning goal.

The result is often *choice paralysis,* sometimes leaving even the most savvy online learning professionals confused about how to proceed. Because the technology is constantly changing, some of it will be new to many who develop online learning materials. Also, it can be expensive (certainly in terms of initial outlay) and require complex skills. Because it is evolving so quickly, the design and delivery technologies can puzzle even seasoned designers.

As a result, many designers simply bow to technological considerations when creating online learning programs—often at the expense of the learning itself. For example, when developing online learning materials, some people choose to show off technological capabilities (i.e., streaming video, audio, etc.) even when these fillips don't add value to a course and may even detract from it.

In other cases, video and audio might augment the learning experience, but learners don't have access to computers or Internet connections that accommodate sophisticated multimedia effects. Remember, video gobbles bandwidth. This now brings us to e-learning *design,* a topic worthy of its own, separate strategy.

What Works

- Know the learner's technical vocabulary and ability.
- Get technical training from an expert.
- Break technical training into small chunks.
- Tame the acronyms.
- Keep it simple.

5 | Orchestrate the Three Sides of Design

The goal of [e-learning] design is to facilitate learning outcomes for a defined audience.
    —DR. STANLEY TROLLIP, director of learning
        solutions, Capella University

 CASE STUDY ▪ First Union Bank

First Union Corporation, the nation's sixth-largest banking company, wanted to deliver online learning to its vast employee and management population. The problem was that population seemed a bit *too* vast. The bank, based in Charlotte, North Carolina, had completed more than eighty mergers since 1985 and had acquired thirty-five other financial entities. The result was a huge, diverse organization of over eighty thousand employees, with a host of different skill sets, ethnicities, and corporate cultures. How to design online training for everyone?

Enter Ninth House Network. In March 2000, First Union partnered with Ninth House as a first step toward achieving its management training goals. "Ninth House is way ahead in their commitment to full-motion video and interactivity," according to Mike Davis, assistant vice president and learning specialist at the bank's New Leadership College. "Some e-learning solutions merely put up text, and the 'e' part is clicking the links to jump around."

Ninth House's training practices are based on the teachings of leading business thinkers such as Tom Peters, Ken Blanchard, and Larriane Segil. Moreover, the company's production and design values are considered among the highest on the market by many clients and industry consultants. Offerings range from simple intranet-hosted, text-oriented refresher courses to full-blown, high-end, interactive multimedia presentations, including eSeries, a TV-like series in which actors onscreen react to situations based on decisions the learner makes.

To date, nearly seven hundred First Union managers have used the Ninth House solution to perfect their management skills. First Union has found that a rich, multimedia solution such as Ninth House's appeals to a new generation of managers and employees raised on video games and simulations. According to Davis, surveys of employees indicate the program has been a huge success. On a scale of 1 to 5 (with 5 being the highest), one course called "Innovation: Wow! Projects," based on the writings of best-selling author Tom Peters, received straight 5s.[1]

FOCUS ON ALL THREE SIDES OF DESIGN—
TECHNICAL, AESTHETIC, AND LEARNING

When we say "design," what does it mean to you? Design is learning (instruction), aesthetics (usability/attractiveness), and technology (the e-delivery). This is the goods. This is where the mouse meets the pad. This is where your online learning lives or dies.

Heather recalls talking to a technical designer once who insisted that visual design in e-learning was not that important. "OK," she replied, "so, what kind of car do you drive?" He owned a gorgeous new sports model, of course. Heather asked, "If it's merely for transportation, why does it need to be so racy and attractive?"

Or how about the times she spent sitting with graphic designers, telling them, "Wow! Yes, that's gorgeous, but it

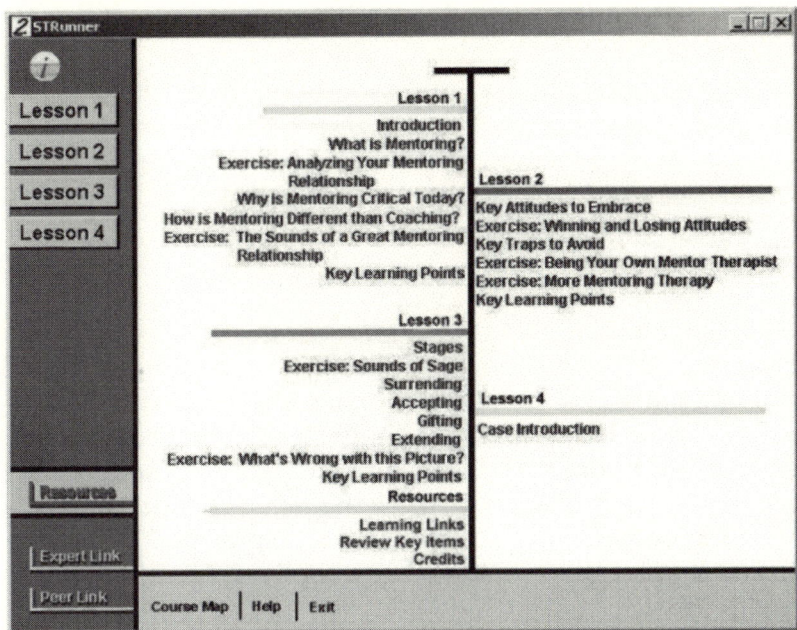

will take too long to download." Or, "It's actually *too* pretty—no one will recognize that as a navigation button." Yes, and working with learning designers to figure out how the three-day course translates into six hours online. (To say nothing of how to structure the pricing. . . .)

Finally, at a recent online learning conference, participants were asked, "How many of you have taken an entire e-learning course or program?" Almost no one raised a hand. And these are the people entrusted with *designing* the stuff?

From our research, interviews, experience, and the introductory case study, we have boiled down the following ingredients for orchestrating all three sides of e-learning design:

- Account for all three sides of design.
- Understand the different learning environments and media.
- Emphasize solid instructional design.
- Beware of user hardware and software limitations.

- Appreciate the nuances of human/computer interface.
- Know when to use graphics.
- Empower trainers.
- Think chunky!
- Be ADL/SCORM-compliant.
- Allow for open architecture.

Take another look at that quote at the beginning of this chapter. Dr. Trollip packs a wallop in that statement—a wallop that all e-learning designers should pause to consider. "The goal . . . is to facilitate learning outcomes for a defined audience." *Defined.* As in *definite.* Specific. That means *know the learner.* As to the verb phrase "facilitate learning outcomes," that means "to help or make easy the transfer of learning." *Facilitate,* literally defined, means to "make easy."

Unfortunately, as the American Society for Training and Development's (ASTD's) Eva Kaplan-Lieserson points out, most instructional designers do the opposite—they make the transfer of learning difficult. Why? "Because they get carried away with technology at the expense of the learning," she states.

Kaplan-Lieserson knows whereof she speaks. As associate editor of ASTD's online magazine, *Learning Circuits,* she's had the chance to observe scores of organizations wrestling with e-learning. The biggest mistake she's spotted to date is this: designers obsessing on learning technologies and forgetting everything they've learned about solid instructional design.

"You've got to put the learner first, not the technology, bandwidth, or infrastructure," she states. "If you start from the perspective of 'What does the learner really need?' instead of 'What technology can we throw at them?' you'll succeed. You want to *engage* learners, not distract them." Ouch. More wallop.

Why this continued emphasis on the learner in a chapter devoted to design? Because as this book goes to press, a new survey from Roper Starch Worldwide reports that the average Web user becomes noticeably frustrated in less than twelve minutes if unable to find what he or she is looking for online. Seven percent begin to despair after only *three minutes* of searching. Designers should keep this in mind when creating their e-learning courses and Web sites; ditto the manager or director rolling out e-learning to the organization.[2]

Does this mean e-learning is an intrinsically new kind of learning experience or simply a more efficient way of filling (virtual) classroom seats? Part of the answer results from the ability to *master* the technology, as we mentioned in the previous chapter. Master, not show it off. It's a matter of aesthetics. Did Gauguin and Van Gogh splatter every color they could think of onto the canvas? Display every tool and technique they'd learned on every painting? *Non.* They painted as simply, as purely, as possible. In a very real sense, they facilitated learning outcomes.

Or, to use another analogy, consider the evolution of stage plays to motion pictures and finally to television. How did the writers, directors, and performers master the communications technology: first the stage, then the big screen, and finally the small screen? Or *did* they?

Tom Kelly of Cisco likens the evolution of e-learning to the development of live stage performances (classroom training) to motion pictures (e-learning). The first "movies" simply used a stationary camera to film the events on stage—regardless of mood, theme, actor movement, and so on. What appeared onstage (mostly) appeared on film. There was no allowance for physical movement or sound, let alone any attempt at interpretation.

But in coming years, astute directors realized that they must bring *reality, or the closest approximation of reality,* to their movies. They created booms and movable cameras to capture the onstage action.

Then came sound, in 1927, with Al Jolson's *The Jazz Singer.* The advent of sound spelled doom for many silent screen stars of the teens and twenties, because they either did not know how to enunciate properly or simply had lousy voices. It also spelled the advent of seasoned, trained, and hitherto undiscovered stage actors who could enunciate and project their voices. Kelly believes that this is where e-learning is today, in relation to movies.

Then came *Citizen Kane*.

"*Citizen Kane*," says Kelly, "showed us how movies *could* be made: the camera angles, close-ups, the lighting—all were revolutionary for that time (1941). Orson Welles presented a tour de force that showed the whole world what movies were capable of."

By the fifties, once the movies were well established (and radio dramas were beginning their slow slide into oblivion), TV came along. At first, no one dreamed that television could supplant the movies in terms of entertaining the masses and delivering quality fare. In the main, they were right. Early television *reeked*—especially the comedies, which were essentially vaudeville performances captured on a single camera, repeating the mistake of the earliest movies.

Enter Lucille Ball. And Ernie Kovacs. And a host of other television innovators. But, with Lucy, a very real and practical consideration gave birth to TV as we know it today: After the birth to her first child, Lucy didn't want to work evenings when comedies were broadcast live; she wanted to stay home with her baby. So, the show was recorded before airing—the first prime-time comedy series to do so.

The production team then saw an opportunity to experiment. Freed from the constraints of live television, the team could use three cameras when recording the show and edit the film afterward. This three-camera approach captured Lucy's stage antics far better than one camera could and eventually became the standard for television comedy thereafter.

Television took another leap forward in the early 1980s with the arrival of *Hill Street Blues* (later mimicked by *NYPD Blue* and *Hospital*), which relied on telling stories primarily through pictures rather than dialogue. The emphasis was on stark realism, conveyed by jittery, handheld cameras capturing the action. It worked.

We believe that e-learning will similarly evolve from the "right on the stage" phase through a Lucille Ball era and into a *Hill Street Blues* or *Hospital* stage. Currently, e-learning programs vary from the "stage" versions (text

converted to html and slapped onto the Web as page turners) to a more *Hill Street Blues*–style approach. This will be
a fundamentally different learning experience, even when
centered around the classroom.

REALIZE TECHNICAL, GRAPHIC, AND LEARNING DESIGNERS ATTENDED DIFFERENT CLASSROOMS

As you develop the objectives for your e-learning program,
always bear in mind the three sides of design: technical (use
it strategically), aesthetic (make it engaging), and learning
(accomplish the objective). Above all, remember that those
involved in each category attended different classrooms.
They have different—and often contradictory—ways of seeing and designing e-learning. A tech-head might not necessarily appreciate your reusable learning object as the final
solution; a graphics guru might not care for the tech-head's
obsession with "preserving bandwidth." As an e-learning
designer, *you* must keep your head while everyone around
you is losing theirs. Kipling would have been an excellent
e-learning guide.

Since Rudyard isn't around these days, however, we will
offer you a guide of your own, so you can choose the most
appropriate contexts to support the e-learning you hope to
achieve. First, let's consider the types of learning environments in most organizations today. While examining them,
keep the three sides of design in mind (technical, aesthetic,
and learning).

- **Traditional training and education**—a structured
  event specifically intended to enhance knowledge
  and skills and in which learning is intentional

- **Embedded performance support**—environments
  designed around a software application in which
  performers receive help from a computer

- **Knowledge management**—systems that capture,
  organize, and share the knowledge of individual
  workers and groups

■ **Collaborative**—technologies that link people in several locations so they can interact with one another

Also bear in mind the two kinds of technology that support e-learning:

■ Technologies for developing the learning program, also called "authoring tools"— the hardware and software used to create learning materials, prepare them for "publication," and administer their use once they are published

■ Technologies for delivering the learning program, including:
  ■ computer hardware (most often a PC) and the software installed on it;
  ■ specialized hardware and software for playing video and audio and for handling complex interactions between the student and the computer; and
  ■ infrastructure—the cables, network interface cards (NICs), and software that connect the computers in a network[3]

In an *ideal* world, you would choose the technology for designing, developing, and distributing e-learning materials *after* you have set your learning objectives and determined the most appropriate context. (All classroom? All e-learning? Some mix of the two?) The technology you choose would be most appropriate to the task at hand and would assist in bringing about the intended results. In short, you would facilitate learning outcomes.

In the *real* world, that rarely happens. Most of the technology used for e-learning is already installed and used for other purposes, such as processing orders, managing computer networks, and storing customer records. Although initial costs may be lower, your choices are limited. Why? Because the technology is also being used by most of the other groups in the organization, such as customer service, human resources, and finance. Indeed, the needs of these groups often curtail the choices of technology for you, the designer.

That's why you must understand the technology infrastructure available in your organization and its compatibility with your learning objectives and context. Then you can adapt it to your needs and make sure that additional technology investments harmonize with what is currently available (another reason why IT partnership early on is crucial).

As you and your organization become more familiar with online learning, you will seek a more active role in choosing hardware and software to make sure the technology is compatible with the goals for e-learning in your organization.

Remember the following five steps when designing an e-learning course, curriculum, or enterprise-wide initiative:

1. **Analyze**—front-end alignment; job and needs analysis
2. **Design**—based on gaps in job skills or knowledge
3. **Develop**—what, where, and how to deliver the course(s)
4. **Implement**—actual delivery of e-learning course(s)
5. **Evaluate**—metrics and measurement (i.e., was learning achieved?)

Phase 1: Analyze
The analysis phase is the basis for all ensuing phases of e-learning design. During this phase, you're taking an X-ray of the organization and seeing how all jobs, tasks, and routines further the organization's business goals. In accomplishment-based curriculum design, this is the "front-end alignment" of the organization, in which we help the client verbalize its business goals, then see how each individual job accomplishes those goals. We do this in order to pinpoint any job, skill, or knowledge problems; identify the source of said problems; and determine possible solutions.

This phase may include specific data-gathering techniques such as job analysis, task analysis, and needs analysis. The product of this phase often includes the instructional goals and a list of tasks to be taught. These "outputs" then become the "inputs" for the design phase.

Phase 2: Design
The design phase involves using the outputs from the analysis to plan a strategy for developing the e-learning curriculum. During this phase, you must outline how to reach the instructional goals determined during your initial analysis and expand the instructional foundation.

Some of the elements of the design phase may include modeling the tasks and behaviors of any accomplished performers identified, conducting a learning analysis, writing objectives and test items, selecting a delivery system, and sequencing the instruction. (And remember all three sides—what are the technical, aesthetic, and learning design requirements?) The outputs of the design phase will be the inputs for the development phase.

Phase 3: Develop
The development phase builds on the previous analysis and design phases. The purpose of this phase is to generate the lesson plans and materials. During this phase, you will develop the instruction, all media that will be used in the instruction, and supporting documentation (job aids, etc). This may include hardware (e.g., simulation equipment) and software (e.g., computer-based instruction).

Phase 4: Implement
The implementation phase refers to the actual delivery of the instruction, whether it's classroom based, lab based, or computer-based e-learning. The purpose of this phase is the efficient and effective delivery of learning. This phase must promote the students' understanding of material, support the students' mastery of objectives, and ensure the students' transfer of knowledge from the instructional setting to the job (Level 3 evaluation).

Phase 5: Evaluate
This phase measures the effectiveness and efficiency of the instruction. Evaluation should actually occur throughout the entire instructional design process—within phases, between phases, and after implementation. As Cisco's Tom Kelly advises, "Measure everything."

The focus of the content and delivery medium should be based on the analysis of the learners, completed in phase 1. The tone of the text, the reading level, the simplicity or complexity of interactions—all should be determined by the needs of the learner.

As in writing fiction, showing is better than telling, and allowing learners to try out a new skill or knowledge—to "play" and experiment—is best of all. This is why increasingly more content providers are incorporating gamelike scenarios instead of the usual hum-drum multiple-choice tests. Allowing students to try out their new learning in a simulation that is a close approximation to reality is best of all. The danger, again, is going overboard: plugging too much interactivity or multimedia into the design. Less is usually best.

Online assessments should provide better alternatives to fill-in-the-blank and "multiple-guess" questions—ideally, a mixture of true/false, multiple choice, and interactivity. Also, mix-and-match questions that allow the user to click and drag the answer to the appropriate match is a solid design choice. "Miniquizzes" should be popped into the course every few screen pages, to keep the student alert and to reinforce learning. Finally, quiz and test questions should feature randomized test items to help ensure test security, and the program should record results to databases for easy tracking and measurement.

APPRECIATE THE INTEGRATION OF TECHNOLOGY AND GRAPHIC DESIGN

As Internet technologies evolve and bandwidth continues to expand, we're seeing an increasing integration of graphic design in e-learning content. This includes everything from "hypergraphics" (featuring html-style "hot spots" within pictures) to full-blown multimedia movies (usually in avi, mpg, ram, or other formats). What's the significance for the e-learning provider and buyer? Two words:

Caveat emptor.

Be very, very careful about the latest, greatest techno-whizbang authoring tool or delivery medium presented you by a salesperson. It may be too much for your network or hardware. If you're on the provider end, be extremely judicious about the amount and complexity of graphic design (streaming video, audio, mpgs, avis, etc.) that you pack into your product offering. Many of your clients may not be able to enjoy it due to hardware, software, or bandwidth limitations.

Despite the breakthroughs in Web-based streaming media, most learners today are still faced with serious bandwidth limitations that result in postage stamp–sized video windows, interminable load times, choppy audio/video playback, and intermittent crashes.

Here are two examples of technology-/graphics-based training program failures as reported by Kevin Kruse of Raymond Karsan Associates, in ASTD's "E-learning 101":[4]

- A large hotel chain completed a $250,000 online learning project only to find out that the computers in their hotels weren't able to run the finished software.

- A major pharmaceutical company invested $1.5 million to create a series of multimedia tutorials to teach human anatomy to their sales representatives. The high-end, 3D animations were truly amazing—and many were amazed again when these animations couldn't be viewed on the three-year-old laptops used by the sales force.

Even the pros at Ninth House have had glitches with technology. All three sides of design are considered, but the client's lack of bandwidth sometime gets in the way of delivery success. In cases like these—and undoubtedly many thousands of others—the project managers need to remember the cardinal rules of Web-based training:

1. Identify the technical limitations of learners' computers early in the process.

2. Design to accommodate the lowest common denominator.

3. Test the design early in the project life cycle.[5]

As Kruse points out, e-learning vendors eager to land new accounts sometimes promise more than they can deliver or you can receive. This is not meant to imply that some sales reps are unscrupulous—quite the contrary: they're often as baffled by technographic problems as the buyer.

During the demo phase of a sales pitch, vendors often show dazzling programs packed with bells and whistles, along with guarantees that the technology used is "standard" or "easily deployed." If you remember nothing else from this strategy, remember this: *Make the sales rep demo the program on* your *hardware, over* your *network.*

There's no doubt that the latest Web technology adds tremendous value for online learning, but if it isn't evaluated carefully, it can become a barrier to program implementation. If you're providing or shopping for e-learning programs for low-end hardware use—but still want at least *some* multimedia applications—we have good news: yes, Virginia, it is possible to develop effective multimedia courses for antiquated or "legacy" systems.

Step 1: Once you've identified the technical limitations of the users' computers, you will know what hardware platform and OS to shoot for—and aim no higher. Design for that level of machine or lower. Higher only comes in after the users' computers are upgraded.

Step 2: When you start the project design phase, concentrate on several key areas:

- **Animation.** Having determined your hardware limitations, consider any multimedia capabilities— when and where appropriate. One element often overlooked is simple animation. Several of today's multimedia authoring tools include animation capabilities that can add pizzazz to your project.

- **Graphics.** Graphics add interpretive sparkle to any learning; they serve to assist comprehension, not detract from it. Solid graphic design doesn't require computers that can display thousands of colors.

In fact, some graphic artists specialize in low-color depth—even black and white—and still produce dazzling results.

- **Interactivity.** Well-designed interactivity is crucial to online learning, especially when delivering over low-end hardware (since you won't have sizzling audio/video effects). If the interactivity is poorly designed, learners will skim through the material or shelve it altogether. Design the interactivity so that learners are *interacting with the content,* not merely the navigation.[6]

So, what does it mean to interact with the content? Most simulation-based learning designs are excellent examples of interactivity. Well-designed simulations encourage learners to make decisions based on the content. The main drawback to simulations is that they can be difficult and time-consuming to design.

Furthermore, they're not always the best choice for all types of training. Here are some common technographic red flags to watch for:

- **Java.** This is a language (not to be confused with JavaScript) that transfers a small program called an "applet" to an end-user's computer. Due to security and virus concerns, many organizations prohibit Java applets from entering the corporate firewall (which renders the training program inoperable).
- **Plug-ins.** These are additional browser-based programs for running Web-based audio or video. If users do not already have them installed, they'll be unable to run the program.
- **Streaming audio and video.** This feature is great when it works, but few companies provide the high-speed bandwidth necessary for it. Most Web-based video still suffers from small viewing windows, dropped video frames, and choppy audio.

From a design standpoint, be sure to provide a strong but simple user interface. When most learners complain about e-learning, it's often not the training they object to

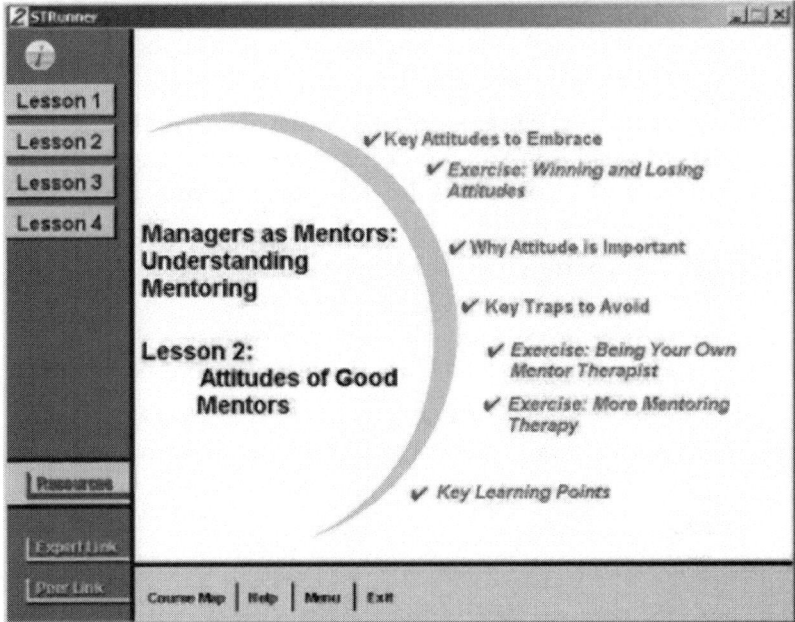

but the confusing menus, unclear buttons, or illogical links. How many times have you been using software or surfing the Web and wondered, "What am I supposed to do now? Did I see everything there is to see? How do I get out of this thing? What's it doing now? Is it hung up, or should I wait longer?"

Probably the single most neglected topic in the field of technology-based training is the interaction between learners and computers. Bad habits in CD-ROM development have worsened as we've moved training to the Web. While you must pay attention to instructional design and technology, don't forget the aesthetics—how learners navigate the system. Solve the most frequent interface problems by using the following tips:

- **Use fewer scrolling windows.** Keep pages short and critical information toward the top of each screen.
- **Go easy on the hyperlinks.** Learners often get lost or confused when jumping from link to link. Consider the use of pop-up windows.

- **Keep your cues consistent.** If you vary a button's location or look, users may assume that they're seeing a new function.

- **Be careful with text formatting.** Since hyperlinks usually appear as blue underlined text, you should avoid underlining regular text for emphasis; use bold or italics instead.

- **Give guidance and feedback.** When in doubt, err on the side of guidance. Make sure all screens show the current page number, lesson, or module title. Error messages should include guidance for fixing the error.

- **Provide a visual history of the learner's progress,** including checkmarks for completed lessons, a bookmark function, and score tracking of assessments.

The integration of technology and graphic design invests e-learning with many powerful tools, but they can actually impede learning if improperly designed or implemented. Most top designers and authoring tools account for what works and what doesn't in e-learning environments. Following these guidelines will help the end user and provider a long way toward guaranteeing Web-based training programs that get real results.

When to Use Graphics

In business presentations, books, reports, e-commerce sites, and similar applications, graphics most commonly represent data. But there are other possibilities. Consider the following uses for graphics:

- **First impressions.** If your company or e-learning site is relatively unknown, graphics can make a splash. Also, learners or visitors outside your firewall must get a good first impression before they delve into the content.

- **Company brand.** People remember graphics and pictures and will associate a logo or a style with your company.

- **Message clarification.** Colors, lines, and other distinctive graphical applications help direct learners' attention to your most important message.

- **Explanations and guidance.** Appropriately used, a picture speaks a thousand words. These features can also help learners navigate your e-learning site.

- **Emotional impact.** Pictures and colors connote different meanings and affect people psychologically. *Caution:* Different colors carry different meanings in other cultures; be sure you know what you're saying with the color you choose.

When Not to Use Graphics

Avoid using graphics unless you have a compelling reason for doing so. Graphics gobble bandwidth, and excessive use will only make your site or company look amateurish. Content will always be the star of your e-learning show, so think of graphics as footlights for that star. They are a way to ensure learners get what they need, just as much as they need, right when they need it.

Also, another trend in the industry is the rise of wireless technology as a venue for e-learning coursework. The next generation of e-learning—already emerging—could well be dubbed "m-learning," or mobile learning, accessible via cell phones or other handheld Internet devices. It's particularly well suited to delivering small chunks of knowledge—*learning objects*—as opposed to entire courses, overburdened with graphics and animation, requiring much bandwidth.

But for those e-learning applications where graphics, streaming media, and the like are appropriate, remember these tips:

- Hire professional graphic designers. Make sure that they are learning-oriented and will be mindful of usability concerns (i.e., file size and average user modem speeds).

- Think about the image you want to project, and design your site according to that image.

- Make sure your graphics don't detract from or obscure the content.

- Beware of copyright and trademark law when "borrowing" ideas from other sites.

- Beta-test your graphics on would be learners. Getting the learner's opinion before deployment is always a good idea.

Content advocates such as Jakob Nielsen are undoubtedly correct in praising content over graphics. Still, it would be foolish to overlook the power of good graphic layout to facilitate learning *and* in reinforcing your company brand.

LET THE TRAINERS TAKE THE LEAD

One of the hottest topics of contention in e-circles today is the issue of who to put in charge of e-learning—the techies or the trainers? Techies are the ones running the show, right? They're the ones already monitoring everything, maintaining the infrastructure, hardware, and software, and generally keeping the whole house of cybercards up, right? Sure. But what do they know about training? Teaching?

Tony O'Driscoll, executive-in-residence with IBM's Institute for Knowledge Management, recently addressed this topic in a witty column for ASTD's *Learning Circuits* online magazine. In O'Driscoll's column, titled "What's Your Web-Based Learning Strategy?", he tackles the question of how trainers, IT staff, and HR personnel can all just get along.

O'Driscoll (among others) suggests that the potential speed and power of the Internet has allowed a kind of "honeymoon" period for training departments and executive management. Executives know they can save time and money with online learning and are willing to give trainers the lead. The only problem is that, historically, the misapplication of new technologies soon sours the honeymoon. However, some key lessons have emerged:

- The majority of technological applications to date have focused on training delivery.

- Most of those applications were devised within the traditional training development model.

- Those technological alternatives were largely aimed at improving training effectiveness and efficiency, as opposed to improving organizational effectiveness and efficiency.

- Although many trainers are aware that most previous attempts to incorporate technology into training have failed, technolust constantly stimulates them to try the latest technological gizmo.[7]

Right now, as O'Driscoll points out, that gizmo is the Internet. Unfortunately, in practice, for many training departments, the 'Net is just a bigger hose with which they spray training at employees and pray that organizational performance will improve. To use the Internet effectively as an *enabler of learning,* and not merely a faster form of delivery, trainers must recognize that their success depends on improved organizational performance—not increased training activity. Once trainers adopt a performance approach, based on inculcating employee accomplishments, the Internet looks and behaves quite differently.

The online learning model that's evolving now puts the learner in the center, networking with peers and seeking information on the Web. To embrace that learner-centered model fully, trainers must understand that the Internet can be leveraged to provide people with just-in-time learning that enhances decision making while improving learners' ability to innovate.

Peer to Peer, or *Everyone's* a Trainer

This leads us to a brief look at peer-to-peer (P2P) content sharing. That's right—as in Napster, gnutella, and aimster. Who would have guessed that the technology used to informally distribute millions of Marilyn Manson MP3s would help government bureau-rats swap stats on bovine methane emissions? (And they do: the government studies everything; cow gas is deemed a major factor in global warming.)

FIGURE 5.1 Typical Government Statistics

1990	1991	1992	1993	1994	1995	1996	1997	1998
58.2	58.1	59.1	59.6	59.9	60.5	60.2	60.2	58.8
32.8	33.2	33.7	34.5	32.7	34.9	34.5	34.2	33.7
33.0	33.4	33.9	34.6	34.3	34.0	34.6	34.1	33.6
15.0	15.5	16.0	17.1	18.8	19.7	20.4	22.1	22.9

P2P file sharing, the technology behind both Napster and gnutella, is moving into offices and cubicles. Even the federal government has a new Web site that uses P2P technology to revolutionize the way it collects, shares, and disseminates statistical data (with only small traces of cow gas involved).

These P2P systems are like Napster with a security code. The renegade music-swapping service used a central directory to steer users to another PC where the desired files were stored. Napster actually stored very little on its server—all the goodies were on other users' hard drives. Technically, Napster didn't nab anything but merely acted as the bookie/traffic cop for illegal music traffickers.

Similarly, the corporate version of Napster, gnutella, or aimster-like technology requires employees to store files on servers, which can then be password protected. Authorized individuals are alerted when new files are added and when they can access them. Same idea, same technology, much less head banging.

In some cases, P2P makes the information being swapped more useful. Government statistics, for example, have until now been . . . well . . . pretty dumb (see the bovine methane emissions studies sometime). Figures on everything from population growth to energy consumption, available to the public on the FedStats.gov portal since 1995, invariably appear as nothing more than numbers on a page—not especially helpful to anyone who wants to know what the data mean (see figure 5.1).

"People want . . . data that they can sort and combine with other data," says Brand Niemann, a computer scientist at

FIGURE 5.2   Improved Government Stats

TABLE ES-9   U.S. SOURCES OF METHANE EMISSIONS (MMTCE)

SOURCE	1990	1991	1992	1993	1994	1995	1996	1997	1998
LANDFILLS	58.2	58.1	59.1	59.6	59.9	60.5	60.2	60.2	58.8
ENTERIC FERMENTATION√	32.7	32.8	33.2	33.7	34.5	34.9	34.5	34.2	33.7
NATURAL GAS SYSTEMS	33.0	33.4	33.9	34.6	34.3	34.0	34.6	34.1	33.6
MANURE MANAGEMENT	15.0	15.5	16.0	17.1	18.8	19.7	20.4	22.1	22.9
COAL MINING	24.0	22.8	22.0	19.2	19.4	20.3	18.9	18.8	17.8
PETROLEUM SYSTEMS	7.4	7.5	7.2	6.9	6.7	6.7	6.5	6.5	6.3
RICE CULTIVATION	2.4	2.3	2.6	2.4	2.7	2.6	2.4	2.6	2.7
STATIONARY SOURCES	2.3	2.4	2.4	2.4	2.4	2.5	2.6	2.3	2.3
MOBILE SOURCES	1.5	1.5	1.5	1.5	1.5	1.4	1.4	1.4	1.3
WASTEWATER TREATMENT	0.9	0.9	0.9	0.9	0.9	0.9	0.9	0.9	0.9
PETROCHEMICAL PRODUCTION	0.3	0.3	0.3	0.4	0.4	0.4	0.4	0.4	0.4
AGRICULTURAL RESIDUE BURNING	0.2	0.2	0.2	0.1	0.2	0.2	0.2	0.2	0.2
SILICON CARBIDE PRODUCTION	+	+	+	+	+	+	+	+	+
INTERNATIONAL BUNKER FUELS*	+	+	+	+	+	+	+	+	+
TOTAL	177.9	177.7	179.4	178.7	181.6	184.1	183.1	183.8	180.9

+ Does not exceed 0.05 MMTCE.
√ Bovine methane emissions (cow gas)
* Emissions from International Bunker Fuels are not included in totals.
Note: Totals may not sum due to independent rounding.

the Environmental Protection Agency (EPA). "That's what we're going to provide." Niemann is one of a select few tech-gurus who are transforming the way the federal bureaucracy publishes and shares its work (see figure 5.2).[8]

Notice the improvement—same numbers, same years, same methane gas, but now the data begin to make sense. Now it is useable. And sharable, peer to peer.

Thanks to P2P technology, the government can now make statistics downloadable into spreadsheets that can be parsed, chopped, sliced, or diced as needed. "We can create new documents and databases that weren't possible before," says Niemann, who is also a member of the federal government's FedStats task force.

P2P will also make collecting data a lot easier for Big Brother. With the technology Niemann's group is using from the firm NextPage, each agency's county representative would enter data on a hand-held computer and copy the file to a local server. The data would be automatically available to everyone else on the system and to the public; every time the file is modified, everyone would see the update. "The potential time and cost savings are enormous," notes Niemann. "And you wouldn't have an annual statistical abstract; it would be a real-time statistical abstract."[9]

That's great for the government, but few companies compile statistical abstracts. Still, plenty of information is stored on individual hard drives—e-mail, spreadsheets, industry reports, jpg and bmp images, news items downloaded from the Web, and so on— that could be shared profitably with colleagues or customers.

The possible benefits to e-learning are enormous: rapid, learner-directed, anywhere-anytime learning on the job— that state of "learnativity" we discussed earlier. Employees would approach the Socratian concepts of learning, working, and doing—all at once.

Today's competitive environment doesn't allow the luxury of time to separate learning activity from work activity. If trainers view the Internet as an enabler of learning within the work context, it can indeed be possible to accomplish work activity and to learn at the same time.

However, trainers would do well to ignore the Internet if they plan simply to "Webify" current training curricula. Ineffective training put on the Internet merely allows trainers to waste people's time more efficiently. As mentioned earlier, certain learning interventions are just not suited to a digital medium. To quote veteran programmer-cum-social-critic Clifford Stoll, "You can't download trust." Any

To print, go to the bottom of this page and click "Print."
To return to the course, click on the "x" at the upper right of your computer screen.

Managers as Mentors: Understanding Mentoring

Analyzing Your Mentoring Relationship

• What words would your protégé use to describe you?

• What are the things about this mentoring relationship that might contribute most to his or her anxiety or nervousness?

• What could you say or do that would help your protégé feel comfortable as quickly as possible?

• Is there anything you can change about the site where you meet or plan to meet that would promote confidence and comfort in your protégé?

team building, diversity awareness, or other experiential learning activity will stand a much better chance of yielding the desired behavior change when delivered in physical rather than virtual space.

A smarter use of the Internet is to automate the components involved in managing online learning. Registration, evaluation, resource management, and reporting can easily be moved to a Web-based model, thus freeing up training department resources to use the Internet to foster a learning culture within the organization. This is why LMSs were invented.

THINK CHUNKY—OBJECT-ORIENTED LEARNING

Decades of testing in the fields of psychology (especially mnemonics), education, and training prove that *most* people learn concepts—even verbal concepts—in the form of objects.

According to the *Encyclopedia of Learning Technology* (http://coe.sdsu.edu/eet/Admin/TOC/), "People think in terms of objects. As we perceive the world, we attempt to pick out 'things,' and then we try to group those things into familiar categories so that we can predict their characteristics or behavior."

We often notice similarities between the objects we see and our mental image of objects that are "typical" of a category. Thus, we naturally make mental associations from the specific (the newly perceived object) to the general (a known object category). We also try to recognize an object's parts and then infer the identity of the object.

For example, we can quickly tag an object with wings, feathers, and a beak as belonging to the "bird" category. (The downside is that we also tend to label people this way, usually based on appearance—e.g., long hair and beard = hippie stoner—completely forgetting the old adage about judging a book by its cover.)

Yet, if we didn't categorize objects, we'd waste a lot of time investigating each new object we encountered. For example, if we couldn't categorize something as poison, we wouldn't know that it was unsafe to ingest without repeated (and painful) experimentation.

In the main, this is how we learn—by association. We associate a new concept, logarithm, and so forth, with a known set of similar objects. We infer meaning, test our association, and confirm whether we are correct. This is the basis for learning objects, or object-oriented learning.

Learning objects have four characteristics:

- **They are self-contained (autonomous)**—they have everything they need in order to appear and behave in predictable ways to stimuli (think of a porcupine or a skunk).

- **They are made up of component parts**—the feathers, wings, and beak of a bird.

- **They belong to a category**—robins, wrens, sparrows, and so on, are all in the bird category; skunks and porcupines are not.

- **They may have subclasses of objects that inherit their characteristics and sometimes add new ones—** a robin lays an egg, within which is a baby robin, inheriting many of the characteristics as the parent object, while adding new characteristics of its own.

RIOs and RLOs

What do objects, categories, and porcupines have to do with e-learning? Every. Single. Thing. As devised and defined by industry leader Cisco, learning "objects" are the fundamental building blocks of an entire e-learning content library. Each learning object is an autonomous component, a "chunk" of learning content designed to be interoperable with other chunks from a wide variety of sources. Thus, it is not only a discrete learning object but also a reusable learning object (RLO) (see figures 5.3 and 5.4).[10]

A good example of an RLO would be a chunk of learning focused on the four steps necessary to defragment your hard drive in Windows 98:

1. Click the Start button.
2. Click Run.
3. Type "defrag."
4. Click OK.

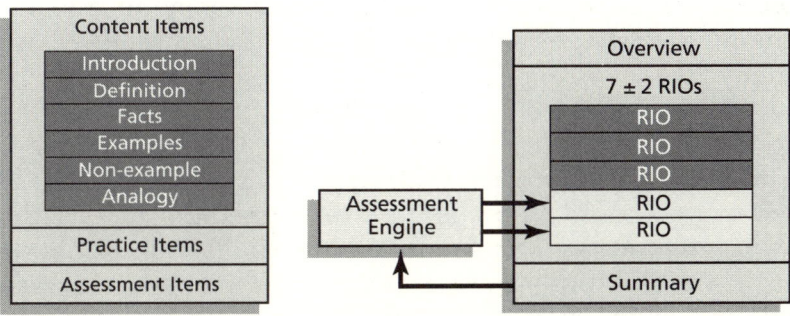

FIGURE 5.3   RIO Model   **FIGURE 5.4**   RLO Model

Such a reusable learning object could be combined with other RLOs to create a lesson or module—even an entire course. It can then be reused with other chunks to form part of a different lesson or course.

As you can see, each RLO is composed of individual steps (information objects), which in turn are also reusable—hence, reusable information objects. These are the smallest chunks of learning that still have meaning to the learner. Think of atoms that, grouped together, form a molecule. The atoms can be grouped and regrouped in different combinations to form different molecules—over and over again, world without end.

Both RIOs and RLOs can be stored in a database and "tagged" using metadata. Metadata is information about an object and can be searched on a Web site or intranet site to find, sort, and retrieve objects. Metadata can be the name of the author, the instructional approach used, or the learning objective it works to fulfill. Think of the Dewey decimal card index file, used to sort and find library books in all libraries that use the Dewey Decimal System. The libraries are the learning content, the books are the RLOs, the chapters of each book are the RIOs, and the card index is the Metadata.

RLOs allow designers to create content *once*, store it in a database using Metadata, and deliver it in *many* different structures, with a variety of components—including text, graphics, video, and audio. This not only allows for customization of content on the fly but also facilitates tracking progress, just-in-time learning, just-as-much learning as well as enterprise-wide knowledge management. And it's the most cost-effective approach to date: create once, use many times.

The glue that holds all this together, in terms of making RLO-based e-learning content, delivery, and use interoperable with everyone's computers and networks, is, of course, standards. As was the case in the early days of the Web, no standards means no compatibility. And, just as html came along—in a standardized format and language—to improve the Web's accessibility, e-learning providers and users will have to adopt a set of standards. And that right soon.

Enter—(wait for it)—Big Brother. That's right: our friends in the government, who created the Internet on the Sixth Day (and saw that it was good), have actually come up with an answer to the perplexing problem of learning object/e-learning standards: the Advanced Distributed Learning (ADL) Initiative.

As described in chapter 4, the ADL Initiative is a collaborative effort among the government's Department of Defense, mainstream industry, and academia to establish a common framework that would permit the interoperability of learning tools and object-based learning content on a global scale. The Office of the Secretary of Defense, the Department of Labor, and the National Guard have established the ADL Co-Lab as a forum for cooperative research, development, and assessment of new learning technology prototypes, guidelines, and specifications.

Open Season

But all of ADL/SCORM's work means nothing without open architecture software. Providers still won't be able to fuse their e-learning software with the end user's infrastructure unless both are open source.

Furthermore, open source software is reliable and inexpensive and allows for modifications. If you've heard of Linux, by Red Hat, you already know something about open source software. Similarly, XML (a scripting language), SQL (a database script), and Apache (a Web server), are all examples of open source software—software code given away for free.

As Patti Shank points out in her article "Open Sesame" for ASTD's *Learning Circuits,* you might not think software that's given away could be worth very much—but you'd be wrong.[11] The Internet would not be where it is today without the open source software movement, as many of the technologies and applications that form the Internet's infrastructure are open source. Hence, the quality and reliability of these technologies is often good.

As Shank points out, open source is not new. Some parts of the UNIX operating system, one of the oldest operating systems in existence, were developed by programmers sharing their source codes. Linux, an open source version of UNIX, is becoming more popular every day. In fact, IBM invested over a billion dollars in Linux in 2001. Thousands of organizations are bailing out of Windows and diving into Linux as their operating system. Even K–12 school systems are jumping on the bandwagon. After all, the code is *free!*

So, what does "free" mean, exactly? Well, the very name itself, "open source," implies that the software is free, but it's more than that: it's freedom to innovate, not just freedom of cost. Programmers are free to modify code, add enhancements, and so forth.

That's a big difference from what computer users are accustomed to. Most proprietary software (and we won't mention any names here [Microsoft]) is provided in a binary executable format that does not allow for modifications, tweaks, or sharing. For instance, when you install Word for Windows on your computer, you don't have access to the code behind the program. All you have access to is an install.exe or setup.exe file that loads Word onto your hard drive.

This binary executable file is only readable by a computer—not by users. Thus, if you need to modify Word's source code to make it integrate with other e-learning software that your organization uses, you're SOL (i.e., out of luck; see the glossary). Although it would be desirable, even necessary, it's impossible and illegal. That's part of the plan—it leaves the market open for software companies to always create *additional* software. Sound familiar now?

Open source developers, on the other hand, will provide the actual source code. If you're knowledgeable enough to read and modify the code, you can; modification is even encouraged. In support, the Open Source Initiative Web site (www.opensource.org) says, "When programmers on the Internet can read, redistribute, and modify the source for a piece of software, it evolves. People improve it, people adapt it, and people fix bugs. And this can happen at a speed that . . . seems astonishing."

By now, you probably see that open source is a good idea—so why would people who develop software give it away? The answer requires a shift in thinking about what you're selling: an object or a service. If you're selling an object (the software), open source is naive. If you're selling a service (support and expertise), open source makes sense. For analysis of the business case for open source software, visit the Kaivo Web site (www.kaivo.com).

Currently, open source applications are just beginning to make their way into the training and education market. As trainers focus on e-learning, the power and flexibility of open source is becoming more apparent—especially if you plan to put your offerings on the world stage.

What Works

- Know technical limitations of learners and their equipment.
- Test the design early in the project life cycle.

Because e-learning is just entering its childhood, instructors may not know all the ins and outs yet. Here are some tips distilled from a host of interviews, Web sites, and industry publications:

- **Be interactive.** E-learners need feedback and encouragement. Provide regular, consistent feedback to both the individual and the group via email, chat rooms, and so on.
- **Be fair and consistent** in your online coaching. Group debate lends itself to various (and contrary) opinions. Try to foster a fair and positive learning environment.
- **Have a backup plan** to make sure your course stays online. Servers go down, and certain operating systems are unpredictable. Allow alternative ways for students to submit class materials (i.e., fax, snail mail, voice mail, etc.).
- **Make sure learners can contact technical support** if problems arise.
- **Be prepared to answer technical questions**, even if this isn't your forte. The goal isn't to become a tech whiz in addition to being an SME but to help e-learners find answers.
- **Be careful of what you post.** You won't get a second chance: your answers/comments are posted permanently, for all to see.

- Everything should be visually appealing and easy to navigate.
- Always keep solid instructional design foremost.
- Don't go overboard on technogoodies.
- Keep an "open" mind.

6 | Think Globally; Learn Locally

You must have increased sensitivity to other cultures. If you just cart American methods and culture into most foreign markets, it's not going to work.

—Jay Cross

 CASE STUDY ▪ Wilson Learning's Global Solutions Group

For a concise, object lesson in how to think globally and learn locally, we've found no better model than Wilson Learning's Global Solutions Group. Headed by Mary Beth Lamb, director, and partner Peter H. S. Bailey, global performance consultant, the group handles globalization issues for a host of Wilson Learning worldwide clients. One recent project for Hewlett-Packard embraced communications issues across multiple cultures in virtual teams.

In addition to teaching skills in conflict resolution, leading virtual teams, and leveraging team versatility, they were able to create an environment where team members from varying cultures, thousands of miles apart, could collaborate in team building. The project was a resounding success, due to the tools and techniques the Global Solutions Group uses every day.

"We have developed tools to help us determine how to design the learning, how to deliver it globally, and how to do post-learning impact analysis," says Lamb. Bailey adds, "The thing to remember is that you cannot solve a problem with the same consciousness that caused it."

Here are their five to do's for achieving success with global learning:

- You must see everything through the "global lens." All the techniques and problems you face when distributing online learning locally, you face to a greater degree when distributing it globally. Examine your global participant base (needs assessment).

- Get someone with expertise in maximizing learning across multiple cultures. One of the keys is understanding the cultural differences that impact learning. Members of your audience are all very different in terms of cultural norms, technology, and existing knowledge. "We're not talking ethnicity," adds Bailey, "we're talking culture, which is a very different thing."

- Maximize participation of diverse peoples as much as possible by way of accelerated learning techniques. Lamb and Bailey estimate that in international communications, 75 percent of the audience is from non-dominant and/or hierarchical cultures; that is, they tend to shy away from dominating conversations or speaking out individually. Two of their Web cast teaching techniques are (1) use written communications (whiteboard) rather than verbal, and (2) break larger online groups (twenty or more) into smaller (five) ones.

- Provide time for people to absorb and process the learning, and account for this added time in the design phase. You may have to minimize the amount of material or number of sessions. Participants need time to assimilate learning.

- Speak to people in their real-world situation, and be careful not to do it all toward any one culture's norms. One example is the communication breakdowns around slang, acronyms, jargon, jokes, and the like. They hinder learning in any environment but absolutely put the brakes on learning in an e-environment. Anything you'd bar in a multicultural environment is even more critical in an e-environment.

Lamb continues, "When going global, apply all these strategies through the global lens—whether it's 'Cater to the Learner' or 'Tame the Technology.' Do your homework."

RESPECT THE WORLD: LANGUAGES, CULTURES, AND CUSTOMS

Have you ever run a search on your browser, found a hit, and followed the link to a Japanese, Chinese, or French Web site?

You back out and follow another link only to end up facing German or Russian language sites. What gives? Doesn't anybody speak English anymore? Well, here's another news flash: English speakers no longer constitute the majority of Internet users. That's right: in May 2001, the balance tilted toward non-English speakers. (If you want to pretend English speakers are still the majority, then *viele Gluck! Buena suerte! Bonne chance!* You are in for a global wake-up call.)

In America, we assume that because the Internet is an American invention all Internet sites are going to accommodate American English. The odd, disorienting sensation we feel when confronted with a foreign-language site is daunting. We may poke about a bit, but we usually can't wait to back out and try another site.

That's the same feeling Internet users in foreign countries experience when they log onto a site and see only English language, characters, and links. The difference is, many of them *can* understand our language to some degree—much more than we understand theirs.

Other countries and cultures speak, write, and post to the Web in their own languages, using their own idioms and colloquialisms. And just as American businesspeople have learned to communicate and negotiate with their counterparts in Asia, Europe, and the Pacific Rim, so must we learn to adapt e-learning to the world.

True, most cultures accommodate English speakers and writers, but not all of them. Remember those midlevel managers in Prague? What if the shoe were on the other foot? What if 90 percent of the Internet sites you wanted to access were in Czech?

Today, more international e-learners are logging on than ever before. GM has employees all over the globe. Ditto Cisco, Ford, and a host of other multinationals. Do you think they serve up only apple pie and vanilla online courses? No way, José.

> "Learning is communicating, and e-learning is e-communicating."
>
> —TOM KELLY

They *think globally and learn locally*. That is, they constantly keep global awareness in mind while designing e-learning and then target it for specific, local audiences around the world. They account for local languages, customs, and idioms before they deliver their online offerings.

Seems fairly self-evident, doesn't it? Yet, you'd be surprised how many other big-name multinationals, with offices and clients scattered all over the world, fail to address cross-cultural communications when delivering their e-learning.

That's right: cross-cultural *communications*. As Cisco's Tom Kelly states, learning *is* communicating. And e-learning is e-communicating.

Are we making too big a deal of this? We don't think so. Just consider a few recent missteps some big-name American companies have made in cross-cultural communications. These are actual advertising messages lost, garbled, or otherwise mangled during translation:

- Frank Perdue's chicken slogan, "It takes a strong man to make a tender chicken," translated into Spanish as "It takes an aroused man to make a chicken affectionate."

- Pepsi's "Come alive with the Pepsi Generation" translated in China as "Pepsi brings your ancestors back from the grave."

- Gerber had problems selling baby food in Africa because it used the same packaging that was so successful in the United States, with the picture of the Gerber Baby on the label. Only later did the company learn that local companies put pictures of a container's contents on the label.

- Coors' slogan, "Turn it loose!" translated in Latin America as "Suffer from diarrhea!"

- The Coca-Cola name in China was first read as "Ke-kou-ke-la," meaning "Bite the wax tadpole" or "Female horse stuffed with wax," depending on the dialect. Coke had to research over forty thousand characters before they found a phonetic equivalent "ko-kou-ko-le," which translates as "happiness in the mouth."

OK, point made. Unless we exercise awareness and care, our e-learning offerings may be misconstrued, misinterpreted, or otherwise *missed* altogether. Does this mean hiring a team of foreign language experts? Investing in Berlitz for business courses? Installing a multilingual translation engine for your Web sites? Or do they even make such things?

Yes, they do. Several American software vendors now offer globalization software that automatically translates your Web sites, e-learning, e-commerce, databases—your entire enterprise—into multiple languages. Furthermore, some of these vendors offer collaboration platforms whereby external users the world over can help fine-tune your content as it hits the Web, allowing you to speak and look like a local firm anywhere on Earth.

This is crucial for any organization seeking entrée into world markets. Today, if you don't speak the lingo, dig the idiom, and case the culture, you're out. Flat. There are just too many other providers who know how to do it. Many of them are European, targeting higher education/e-learning partnerships. And they're quickly closing the gap with their American competitors.

While it's true that most Internet innovators and providers have U.S. Web sites, the rest of the world is catching up. France, Britain, Sweden, and Norway, in particular, are proving fertile fields for developing and implementing e-learning technologies and users. Even though e-learning and Internet use in general is lower in other parts of the world—notably, Africa and Latin America—the burgeoning improvements in international infrastructure and PC accessibility to more people bodes well for the future of global e-learning.

Heather is executive director for the Canaan Foundation, a nonprofit organization that brings computers into rural Kenya. The foundation is bringing technology to parts of the world where it has never been seen before. The students in local schools are learning on the computers to advance their business skills and career opportunities. Today, many organizations go to India to have access to hundreds of programmers who can assist in major conversion of information to e-learning. In the future, we could be going to Kenya instead.

Emarketer.com predicts that by 2004, China will have nearly as many Internet users as Japan, which today is home to about 36 percent of Asia's Internet population.[1] In addition, reports from TrainingZONE and other global e-watchers show that online learning is becoming increasingly popular in the United Kingdom (though classroom training still accounts for most of the education and training there). Still, the message is clear, according to Tim Pickles, TrainingZONE community director: "The proportion of companies using various forms of online learning showed a dramatic rise from 61 percent in 2000 to an anticipated 85 percent in 2001."[2]

The European Commission (EC) in April 2001 adopted a $13.3 billion "E-learning Action Plan" to promote the development of online education by European universities. The three-year plan aims at broadening digital literacy in Europe and reducing the continent's shortage of trained IT workers.

"Europeans must be put into a position very soon of being able to take advantage of the opportunities offered by information and communication technologies," according to Viviane Reding, EC commissioner of education and culture and the plan's main proponent. She said the plan would "enable everybody to continue learning, irrespective of age, and reduce the current skills shortage in the European economy."[3]

The plan envisions communication technologies like digital television and satellites playing a larger role in European higher education and lifelong learning. The document also calls for equality of digital access for all European universities. It says that institutions in economically deprived areas will receive financial and practical help to set up the infrastructure they need to use emerging technologies.

For universities that already are well equipped with information technology, the e-learning plan is likely to result in a greater flow of European Union research money to their computer and education departments. The plan also endorses research on "virtual campuses" and simulation technologies that could provide "access to education resources without constraints in terms of time or space."[4] The plan comprises four main planks:

- Improvement of infrastructure and equipment to be completed by 2004
- A teacher-training drive to take place at all educational levels, with online learning platforms in place in 2002
- Development of content and equipment a top priority
- K–12 schools and colleges to be linked in networks.

The EC's vision? "Improving basic skills, particularly IT, and digital skills, is a top priority to make the [European] Union the most competitive and dynamic knowledge-based economy in the world," European leaders said in a statement at the end of the summit. "This priority includes education policies and lifelong learning as well as overcoming the present shortfall in the recruitment of scientific and technical staff."[5]

The e-learning policy not only is expected to accelerate the spread of educational and training programs (including intellectual property protection for authors) but also calls for increased cooperation among software publishers.

Currently, the e-learning market in Europe is worth about EU12 billion a year (U.S.$10.7 billion)—and growing.

Indeed, the world's first completely online graduate degree comes from the same city that gave us the Beatles: Liverpool. Liverpool University began offering Europe's first purely online degree in IT skills, beginning in 2001. There is no residency requirement, which means people can take the master's degree in information technology and still keep their jobs. The university hopes this will help businesses address the IT skills gap from within their own staffs.

This also means workers in the United Kingdom can broaden their employability without uprooting themselves to go back to college. Although the students never meet in person, they enjoy a "virtual classroom" environment of twenty or so, and they are each assigned a personal tutor. The students and tutors communicate by e-mail, supporting each other and sharing ideas, with access to a twenty-four-hour help desk to handle any technical issues.

Liverpool U delivers the entire course via the Internet, with weekly assignments based on a course textbook and assessment through personal and group assignments. Completion of the degree takes an average of eighteen months to two years, with eight to twelve hours of study each week.

"This course is aimed at professionals who are already working, who have probably had five years work experience and really know why they want to do this—not just for fun or as a social experience," according to Liverpool University vice chancellor Peter Goodhew.

The course, designed by the Dutch firm KIT eLearning, gives people who can't take time off work the chance to gain a postgraduate degree without ever needing to visit a university campus," according to KIT chairman Shai Reshef. "They can study when and where they want and gain the recognition they deserve for their experience."[6]

The cost is currently $12,000 (about £8,000), which Liverpool U says means a big saving on traditional, campus-based courses, with no loss of earnings.

The significance? That European providers and end users are rapidly closing the IT skills and infrastructure gap with their American counterparts. What can American e-learning designers and providers learn from this? And how can they stay in the spotlight on the global stage?

Our advice: start thinking about globalizing your offerings from the get-go, not *after* they're written.

IDC senior research analyst Sheila McGovern reports that the European e-learning market is forecast to grow by 126 percent during 2001, reaching $5.877 billion by 2005. The numbers worldwide are even more impressive. According to Brandon Hall, globalization of e-learning is fast becoming a major trend as organizations in Europe, Asia, and South America embrace the new technology. "Experts estimate that the European market is about twelve to eighteen months behind the U.S. in terms of adopting e-learning," says Hall. "But it is catching up quickly. IDC predicts that the worldwide corporate e-learning market will exceed $23 billion by 2004, representing a CAGR [compound annual growth rate] of 68.8 percent from 1999 through 2004."

Hall believes that North America will likely account for about two-thirds of that growth, but Western Europe will experience the fastest growth rate at 97.2 percent, followed by Japan, Latin America, and the Pacific.[7]

Given the increasing emphasis on global commerce and communications in recent years, the implications are staggering. Literally hundreds of millions of potential e-learners are already poised over their keyboards, utensils in hand, ready for e-dinner.

EMBRACE CROSS-CULTURAL FUNCTIONALITY

Just as we saw how to Cater to the Learner in strategy 1, we will now examine how to Cater to the International Learner. The same rules apply, but with added sensitivity for cross-cultural functionality—understanding the nuances of attitudes, phrases, fonts, colors, and more, in whatever culture you'll be catering your e-learning fare. For example, did you know that:

- in Brunei the color yellow (text, graphics, borders, etc.) denotes royalty? Using yellow implies the official sanction of the king or queen.
- certain Latin American cultures see Help files as mildly insulting?
- many Asian cultures try to avoid saying no directly. The phrase "We agree with much of what you say" can imply "But we won't go for it."
- there is no word for *no* in Thailand?
- American idioms such as "touch base with you" or "phone tag" are incomprehensible to most non-English-speaking cultures?

When creating or disseminating any e-learning fare, first make sure your audience will receive it as intended. Fonts, colors, graphics, sounds, phrases, and attitudes carry different connotations in different cultures. Have you ever tried developing a course in different languages? Sometimes something as simple as straightforward translation gets in the way. Because of technical limitations when merely changing fonts, that information no longer fits.

Or when working with one multinational client who wants a suite of courses translated into Spanish, the question is, *which* Spanish? From Spain or Mexico? Oh, you're going into *South America.* What about Portuguese? And don't forget different time zones, especially when delivering synchronous or live e-learning. How to foresee and account for all these variables?

In *Multimedia for Learning,* Stephen Alessi and Stanley Trollip suggest three potential trouble spots for international e-learning: (1) language, (2) culture, and (3) time.[8]

Some societies are verbal, some are not; some are collaborative, some more private; some put the expert on a pedestal, while others like to attack the expert as part of the learning process. E-learning has to have not only a technology but a methodology, which must be *culturally appropriate to each location*. Sounds again like Cater to the Learner—wherever the learner is.

OK, so how do we do that?

"You ask the workforce or your contacts," says Lamb. "They'll tell you, 'Tell me how people learn in your country,' and listen closely to your affiliates and your customers."

As to specific problem areas, the language barrier obviously is the most pronounced (pun intended). If you're writing e-learning courses for a Saudi Arabian audience, you'd better know how to write Arabic—as read and spoken in Saudi Arabia. Most word processors come with foreign fonts and characters, but you'll need someone fluent in the language to actually compose the text. Again, globalization software can automate the task, but such software carries a price. For example, Heather worked on a training program in Jakarta. One section was in listening. The translation came back as "hearing"—a subtle but important difference when teaching skills.

Less obvious are the cultural differences—idiom, colloquialisms, customs, and norms. For foreign users accessing your site, make sure to use multilingual entry pages, graphic and verbal icons rather than text, and avoid using American slang or jargon. For example, in one college freshman English 101 course, the professor described Hamlet's dilemma as "a real bear," which the American students understood but which left one Russian-born student utterly bewildered.

Finally, there is the prosaic but very real international factor of time zones. One of our clients had each of her direct reports in a different time zone and country. So, what time do you call the meeting? Ever miss a meeting because you thought it was called for the time zone you're in? We have. The more widely dispersed your users, the greater the problem—especially with synchronous training. Here are a few guidelines for trotting your e-learning onto the world stage:

- Look into globalization software or other automated translation platforms.

- Language, culture, idiom—learn it for each audience (think globally; learn locally).
- Account for time/seasonal differences as you do language/cultural ones in your design.
- Avoid references to climate, time of day, or the seasons (which are reversed between the Southern and Northern Hemispheres).
- Use no Americanisms (slang, jargon, etc.).

If you really want to bring the world to your desktop—and vice versa—remember that the *e* in e-learning does not stand for English. Think globally; learn locally. By "locally," we mean providing content in the language and idiom specific to the e-learner's locale. As Carolyn Sostrom, of J@pan-Inc.com, points out, first impressions speak volumes.

"If a company is spending thousands or more on e-learning software or related tools," says Sostrom, "but the content or Web site isn't intelligible, all that happens on the receiving end is downtime."[9] (And a search for new vendors.)

Smart localization means that users in a foreign country see your e-learning as having the language and characteristics of a product developed in that country. This could include using appropriate address, date, and time formats in an online quiz, to moving the steering wheel from one side of the car to the other in a graphic or interactive simulation.

Globalization and Localization Trends

Organizations are facing the challenges of working globally more than ever. In training we wonder whether the facilitator can speak the local language . . . if the case studies are relevant . . . if the videos will work . . . oh, no, how does that work *online* now?

In the late 1970s and early 1980s, "internationalization" meant installing an international keyboard for a computer sold in Europe. Then, software providers and other high-tech companies that had a high level of overseas sales started looking into software globalization and localization, according to Benjamin Sargent, director of marketing communications for Lionbridge Technologies, a provider of multilingual content management products and services.

"In the late 1990s, it started making sense for high-tech companies to have multilingual Web sites," says Sargent. "Then lots of financial services companies and life sciences and medical products companies came on. Now, we're starting to see manufacturing companies going through e-business implementation. They're already global companies, and they're not interested in software or Web localization per se but need global content management as part of an e-business process."[10]

As more companies investigate global opportunities and growth, the need for localization and outsourced expertise increases, according to Tom Shapiro, VP of sales and marketing for Rubric, a localization provider to IT companies. "There is a definite trend toward globalization of *all* businesses, especially information technology companies whose products can be applied so easily on a global basis."

Corporate America, however, doesn't appreciate localization as part of a strategic plan, according to Hans Fenstermacher, founder and president of ArchiText, a software localization provider. "Rather than embracing it, or seeing it as a way to get into a market, it's seen as a stumbling block." He believes American providers, especially, should always plan any product with an eye toward localization sometime down the road.

"Just because you're on the Web doesn't mean your product is global," Fenstermacher adds. He is right in more ways than one: it's not just a matter of international Web sites but international users. According to the *Computer Industry Almanac,* nearly 60 percent of all Internet users now live outside the United States. Which means that localization is no longer an optional, value-added service you slap on if you can afford it—it's essential.

Akihiro Hompu, president of TRADOS Japan, believes that anyone seeking entrée into global markets should use *one* localization provider, in order to ensure consistency. He makes a good point: hiring multiple localization providers to handle a corporation's various multinational divisions is a

guaranteed way to earn an ulcer. Keep it simple. One localization provider for *all* divisions, wherever they may be.
Hompu also suggests that companies should view their
translations as a corporate *asset,* not a burden, and have
one person in charge of managing it, rather than leaving it
in the hands of some translation service.

Technological standards that can make the localization
process run more smoothly continue to evolve. The Unicode
standard assigns a unique number to every character
across all major languages. In a case study performed in
2000 by Forrester Research on Amazon.com's Japanese
storefront, use of Unicode was cited as one of the reasons
for Amazon's success.

Many Asian languages, including Japanese, have more
than six thousand characters. Encoding all these characters in software is far more difficult than encoding Western
alphabets. Amazon also hired outside specialists and kept
content creation local with a centralized software infrastructure—other reasons listed for their success.

"Firms that start with an internationalized palette of
software tools can more easily tailor content delivery to the
needs of a local market," according to the case study. "Amazon alters its bestseller list to suit local culture."

Tips for Localizing E-learning

You've done the research and decided that your e-learning
program or process will work in China, Germany, or Sweden. You recognize the importance of localizing your content, rather than expecting your future learners to read a
different language or understand local idioms and expres-
sions. Now what? What steps can you take to achieve success in your localization efforts? Here are some suggestions:

- **Research any country/city before designing content.** "Have real discussions before you begin localizing," says Norihisa Ando, of Satyam Japan.

- **Autotranslation can't replace human translation.**
  Language is elastic and always changing. Even

within English, we can barely keep up with the vocabulary.

- **Build the right international e-learning development team.** Don't give someone whose experience is limited to Europe the responsibility for Japanese sales. Fit the right people to the right cultures.

- **Sharpen text in the source language before starting the localization process.** The better written and clearer the text, the easier it will be to translate and the faster it will go. Make sure the words count, and get rid of local slang.

- **Dispose of surplus files so you don't localize junk.** Some providers offer software and tools to help do this.

- **Create a consistent glossary for translators.** Translators should use consistent terminology. We worked with one company designing a "listening" training program. In the Indonesian dialect used, however, the word meant "hear." Although the meaning is close, it has a different intent.

- **Find a provider with a solid localization strategy and a scalable infrastructure.** "You need a provider that can customize for your particular situation," said Tom Shapiro, of Rubric. "You need to know that they are responsive and flexible and that they can nimbly respond to your needs."

- **Combine different players in the design stage early on.** People creating user manuals and online help text should work together so they have consistency in their terminology—this can help save money and time later.

- **Don't think project to project; see globalization as an ongoing project.** "Every project used to be managed separately, with a beginning, middle, and end," says Ben Sargent, of Lionbridge Technologies. Now, people are starting to think of business processes that span several countries at once, instead of a project-to-project approach.

- **Create design with globalization flexibility up-front.** It may cost more at the outset, but it's easier to prepare it for other countries.
- **Involve your foreign office early in the process.** "Get your local office involved in preproject planning and kick-off meetings," said Michael Shannon, of Mendez. "This will help you know your market and understand your final client."
- **Don't forget quality control.** Get someone who knows your industry to perform quality control and assurance.[11]

Trends for the Future

As the Web and wireless e-learning make training and e-learning products more readily available worldwide, the demand for content localization will continue to grow as more companies expand in global markets and hire local employees.

IT'S CALLED WORLD WIDE WEB FOR A REASON

It's already happened, and a lot sooner than most thought it would. Sometime in May 2001, an Internet user somewhere in Asia tipped the global online population in favor of those who do not speak English or for whom English is *not* the mother tongue.

No one saw it coming this fast. Since its inception, the Internet has been dominated by English speakers: programmers, Web site designers, e-commerce providers, hosts, URLs, and so forth. As recently as spring 2001, analysts at U.K.-based market research firm Global Reach estimated that, by 2003, there would be 230 million Internet users worldwide who speak English and 250 million who speak an Asian language, with the tilt toward non-English speakers coming sometime late in 2002. They were eighteen months off. That's how fast the Internet is growing around the globe.

Forrester Research analyst Eric Schmitt notes that "since 50 percent of all online sales (e-commerce, e-learning, etc.) will be outside the U.S. by 2004, a multilingual site is critical." While senior executives often speak English, middle managers may be less at home pursuing online relationships in their second language.

A growing band of "localization" companies, such as Lionbridge Technologies Inc., SDL International (www.sdlintl.com), Globalsight (www.globalsight.com), and Idiom (www.idiominc. com), promises help. They use database-driven software and collaborative systems to translate between English and other languages and to ensure that Web content is culturally sensitive and legally safe.

In diversity or "sensitivity" training, the emphasis is not so much on intercultural literacy as it is intercultural *competence*. This means being aware of interpersonal and intercultural differences and using that awareness as a guide to primarily verbal communication (i.e., stepping through the minefield). But in the text-heavy world of online learning, intercultural literacy is at least as important as competence. Whoever designs your e-learning modules, lessons, and curricula *must* be literate in the language and culture for which the learning is intended.

And there's no time to waffle; international competitors are already collaborating to develop effective cross-cultural e-learning. In Tokyo, Waseda University is actively introducing and applying multimedia and Internet technologies in the classroom environment. In partnership with fourteen other international universities, Waseda launched an aggressive digitalization project called "Cross-Cultural Distance Learning" in 1996. The CUSeeMe-based system offers instant chat with other students around the world.

The aim of this project is, first, to construct mutual understanding and friendship between students of Waseda University and those of its overseas universities. Second, it aims to develop an effective method for the acquisition of English as a common language, as well as other foreign languages. To attain these goals, Waseda is using the latest multimedia and Internet technologies, such as video conferencing, chat, and e-mail systems.

Participating students are thus able to "meet" their overseas partners, exchange views, and learn more about different cultures, societies, and languages, while furthering their academic careers. Waseda University, founded in 1882, now enjoys ties with over 140 universities and learning centers in thirty countries. More than one thousand exchange students currently study at the university.

Despite the industry's recent emphasis on cross-cultural competence, English is still boss on the 'Net. Indeed, most Internet-savvy multinationals make English a main course in their e-learning menus, even though European, Middle Eastern, and a host of Asian companies are rapidly accessing the Internet—which gives rise to an amusing paradox. As more foreign companies enter the market and more Asians go to work for them, the latter may actually *increase* demand for English language and fluency courses.

The Internet, like life, is rife with irony.

What Works

- Remember, it's a small world after all.
- Proof for cultural matches and glitches, with local learners.
- It's about time; it's about space.
- Think globally; learn locally.
- Think again.

7 | Partner with Purpose and Passion

Successful partnerships are not built on deals and contracts. They work because of the heart and soul of the relationship.
—J. W. MARRIOTT, JR.

Honest differences are often a sign of progress.
—MAHATMA GANDHI

 CASE STUDY ▪ FamilyEducation Network

Jonathon Carson, CEO of FamilyEducation Network (FEN), an online education resource for parents, says his firm learned early on that the art of the dance is making relationships work.

"When we started FamilyEducation Network in 1990, we understood that we would have to build our business on carefully chosen and sensitively nurtured strategic alliances. Along the way, we have learned many valuable lessons about what makes strategic partnerships work. What's most important, we have found, is that they're all about relationships."

A few of FEN's partners include the National PTA, the National Education Association, and such corporations as America Online, textbook publisher Harcourt General, and microchip manufacturer Intel.

"A strategic alliance means that the two partnering organizations are involved in something that is of deep importance to both. It's an

151

ongoing, operating relationship. We've tried hard to stay clear of mistakes we've seen many other entrepreneurs make."

According to Carson, the things that successful partnerships *don't* do are (1) thinking too small and (2) thinking only of what the potential partner can do for your company.

"Strategic alliances have to create a situation where both parties gain something; otherwise, they're not partnerships. Too often, an entrepreneur asks the potential partner for an endorsement in return for putting the partner's logo on the company's Web site. That's not strategic."

Carson offers these tips about what successful partnerships *do* do:

- **Build on trust.** Strategic alliances are all about relationships because they're built on trust, dedication, and mutual interests.

- **Have a give and a get.** Each party has to give something and get something in return. When you're the seeker, be clear about what you have to offer the potential partner. "With our corporate partners, money is the prime issue: how can we enhance each other's growth and profitability? Our investors get equity in our company and, if they are major investors, membership on our board," Carson says.

- **Make a commitment.** Each party has to be prepared to dedicate resources to the other. "For example, we've devoted staff positions to working with our association partners. And we expect our partners to assign skilled and competent people to us as well," Carson notes.

- **Be patient.** Strategic alliances take time to develop and time to maintain. Figure out how to stand out from the crowd.

- **Ensure participation at the top.** If the top people in both organizations aren't supporting the goal and working with you, then it's not strategic. The point of any strategic alliance should be to make an impact, and you can't do that without the active engagement of the top people of the organizations involved—yours included.

- **Listen.** Be all ears. Listen to your potential partners. What they tell you will not only give you clues to their needs but may influence your thinking in ways you've never even imagined.

Carson further advises that any successful relationship, e-learning, traditional training, whatever, requires mutual trust and a commitment to seeing both sides come out winners. "Choose your partners with these goals in mind, and you'll quickly discover how much more you can accomplish within a strategic alliance than you could ever do on your own."

PREPARING TO PARTNER

In the scramble to find the "right" e-learning formula or magic, many players increasingly rely on partnering to achieve the desired mix. But when should an organization partner with a vendor, or vendors, and when should a vendor partner with yet other vendors? Or—*gasp!*—even a customer?

Call it outsourcing, partnering, forming strategic alliances, enacting mergers or acquisitions, but linking one's skills (and fate) with another's is simply the way to do business today. With whom do we partner? Seems like almost everyone—vendors, suppliers, customers, internal partners, external partners, and people across the cubicle, down the hall, or around the world.

The e-learning industry is evolving so rapidly that such alliances form, re-form, and split apart again at a bewildering pace. It's like looking under a microscope at amoebae swallowing each other, dividing, moving on. Some flourish and grow, some disappear, and some just bounce around. Since the theme of this book is to offer solid, core business strategies for e-learning success—rather than focus on the ever-changing technologies—let's take a no-nonsense look at sound *business reasons* for partnering in the e-learning arena: when, where, how, and why to form successful alliances.

What is a partnership anyway? We use the word daily but seldom if ever reflect on what it means. A partnership is the blending of strengths for mutual benefit. OK, let's understand what that means. There are some key insights to the definition. "The blending of strengths." This means what do we/I do really well? What's my competitive or strategic advantage? What's valuable or attractive about me?

Then, in looking for a partner, I want someone whose strengths complement mine. Often, in partnerships that fail, the trouble begins here: "Hey, you bake? So do I! Let's start a restaurant!" Oops! No one knew how to do budgeting or marketing.

Or, "My business is having problems with our sales force and so is yours—let's partner." Can you say "Bye-bye"?

Great partnerships come from the combination of *strengths*: "Our alliance with DigitalThink provides a unique and powerful combination class technology and more than thirty years of human performance improvement success that can be delivered in ways that meet customers' requirements," says Gayle Kirkeby, president of Wilson Learning Corporation. "This strategic alliance will integrate DigitalThink's recognized leadership in e-learning with our proven content."

Makes sense. Wilson is known for its legendary global classroom-based work and content, while DigitalThink is recognized for the strength of its technical developmental abilities. Gayle also commented that the organization's and management team's values were aligned.

OK, let's look at this "mutual benefit part." Who is winning at your marriage or other relationship? No one, we hope. It should be equal. Same thing in great partnerships. There are no winners or losers. It is about combining energy forces to be mutually great and bring valued benefits to all. So, what is successful partnership?

A successful partnership is a relationship based on trust plus a clear agreement on, and passion for, the goal.

Steve McMillen, vice president of executive leadership development at Hillenbrand Industries, has some insightful and practical thoughts on organizations partnering with e-learning providers:

- **Avoid the bake-off.** Be very clear about what you need from your partner. Many organizations have "beauty pageants" in which potential partners parade through with all their bells and whistles. Do your homework. Know what you need and have them present to those needs.

- **Show me.** First, you must define what you are looking for in e-learning and what you truly need from a partner. "Start by talking," McMillen advises. All vendors say they are world leaders. Step back from the sweetness and say, "Show me." There is a tendency in the technology and the consulting business to say, "Sure, we can do that." Perhaps they can, but you should ask the question in terms of *results* instead of *beliefs*.

- **Understand the real costs.** The focus is usually on the financial, but there are also huge hidden costs in terms of emotional trauma going into the installation. Account for the wear and tear in the process. Be sure to ask the questions that will help you understand how the partners are going to work together.

- **Be honest and push back.** Find someone who will say, "I understand that you want to do XYZ, and we can do that, but you are barking up the wrong tree." You want a partner who will challenge you, help you grow, and reach the right decision rather than get caught up in the mumbo jumbo of partnering for the sake of partnering.

- **Be aware of the dark side of e-learning.** Many of us come to e-learning from the training or O side. We get intimidated by the technology. *Embrace your own* *ignorance.* Get clear on definitions. The "go-live" date to you might mean something completely different for the supplier. Learn the terms.

- **Check pedigrees.** Look at the "families." Do they come from a learning organization or technology background? Most organizations lean to one side. They both may be able to meet your need, but it is important to know the orientation and things they will miss or stress.

- **Realize it's just the beginning.** The best of the best are a chapter ahead. The application of e-learning is just beginning. Get a partner to enjoy and explore the quest with you. It's an exciting time to look closer at the learning application as well as being enamored by the technology.

- **Realize it's about change.** We often forget that it's about *development.* It is not about bits and bytes and zippy programs. It's about learning and intervention. We get collective amnesia when we put an *e-* in front. It's not about the executive assessment based on competencies and linked to our LMS but about the result of behavior change we are looking for the assessment to drive.

- **Beware of the buzz.** LMS, LCMS, ASP, whatever the hot term of today is—don't be mesmerized by words and hype. What do you want your LMS to do? Is it strategic, transactional, or enabling?

- **Jump into the pool.** Do *something.* The industry is evolving fast. Someday soon it will be like plumbing. Houses for sale don't promote the fact that they have plumbing; it's *expected.* E-learning will become a part of the fabric of our life. You need to get into the pool.

Using these guidelines has helped McMillen guide Hillenbrand into solid, mutually beneficial e-learning relationships with a select group of vendors, content providers, and technology services providers to enhance human performance and reach business goals.

WHAT SUCCESSFUL PARTNERSHIPS ARE

Boyd Clarke, CEO of the Tom Peters Company, advises organizations to pay attention to a potential partner's future prospects. Because of the current chaos of shifting alliances, clueless newcomers, dot-com shakeouts, and mass consolidation underway, it's a tricky business. "Chances are nine out of ten that, no matter who you choose, they're going to be out of business in a year or two. But we must choose anyway. My first rule is this: A good partner understands that *sweet spot where learning theory meets the Internet.* Some do; most don't.

"Second, they have to deliver at a speed and price point that's going to work for you." It doesn't have to be the fastest or the least expensive, but it must be a solid fit in both categories for your organization.

"Thirdly, design and quality: they have to provide MTV pizzazz on CNN timing. We're competing for mindshare, so it has to be *wow.* Learning theory and the Internet are part of that *wow.* Most importantly, you should look at their balance sheet, see how stable they are."

Boyd draws an analogy between the e-learning industry of today with the railroad industry at the turn of the twentieth century. "In 1880 there was more track laid for railroads than in any decade in history—but in the 1890s more railroads went out of business than in any decade in history. I think we're seeing that starting to happen with e-learning. Yet, the railroads roared along for decades afterward; they were just consolidated."

Samantha Chapnick at Research Dog expands on Clarke's second point: the good fit. "If you're right for me," she says, "we're going to be successful and have a great partnership." Chapnick adds that one reason partnerships fail is because members are somewhat less than totally forthcoming. "People today are so afraid of alienating others that they'll keep criticisms to themselves rather than risk upsetting a partner, vendor, or customer." But an honest, *healthy* "fit," she insists, is more important than anything else—including price/speed, technology, or brand.

It goes back to the strength thing. Know what you do well and what you don't. Be open about what you need help with. If you did *everything* perfectly on your own, you wouldn't be looking for a partner. What's the magic that the synergy brings?

"People are partnering with those *who give results* with minimal aggravation," says Chapnick.

In *Dance Lessons: Six Steps to Great Partnerships in Business and Life,* Heather and her partner Chip Bell compare business partnerships with the intricate art of dance. As they point out in a recent article based on their book, partnering is the critical success factor of almost all relationships in today's world of enterprise. "Organizations are fast becoming fluent in the language of mergers and strategic alliances, yet fifty-five percent of business alliances fall apart within three years—75 percent due to incompatible corporate cultures and 63 percent due to incompatible management personalities."[1]

No matter how compelling the e-learning need or how convincing the business rationale, it will be a failure statistic rather than a success without getting the "heart" and "soul" right. Here are six "take it to the bank" protocols or commitments key to partnership greatness:

- **Great partnerships *expect the best.*** This standard not only serves as a criterion for achievement but also provides a noticeable self-fulfilling optimism. Partners enter the relationship with optimism, hope, and conviction that all will go well.

- **Great partnerships work to *be all there.*** They bring a perpetual energy to every encounter. When they are there, they are *all* there. Never lazy, disinterested, or indifferent, they are curious when they listen, animated when they contribute.

- **Great partnerships *assert the truth.*** This proactive gesture keeps integrity at the forefront of all dealings. Their use of unabashed candor triggers improvement and trust.

- **Great partners *honor their partner.*** Honoring is made of admiration and respect. It is also made of the valuing of unique differences.

- **Great partnerships *keep their promises.*** Trust is the glue of partnerships. Reliability is the foundation of trust. Stay honest. Hold on to your integrity and authenticity.

- **Great partnerships *stay—on purpose.*** Partnerships require resoluteness and tenacity to the mutual goal or dream. It entails the "hang in there" side of commitment. The "stay" part is a dogged determination to stay the course despite inevitable bumps and hiccups.

Strategic alliances rise and fall based less on their business rational and more on the success of their synergy. Many are fair; great ones are rare. Great partnerships succeed because they have *soul.* Passion. And the soul of partnership is allegiance to the above six core protocols that direct the rhythm of the relationship.

Paul Earl, CEO of Interactive Technologies, Inc., has some pointed advice about e-learning partnerships: "Partnerships are definitely the way to go. Anyone trying to do it all internally might succeed with the first initiative, but then the whole job of keeping it all up-to-date (customers, technology, content, etc.) just gets to be too overwhelming."

WHAT SUCCESSFUL PARTNERSHIPS DO

In the field of e-learning, successful partnerships do more than swap expertise for pay; they work together in symbiosis, growing with each other and sharing the risk: the vendor provides, the client learns and provides feedback; the vendor learns and provides more. Both grow, share the risks of such growth, and improve.

Scott Sutker, IT Manager for First Union Bank, in Charlotte, North Carolina, advises organizations to "start small where you can build on early successes. Then make your vendors become business partners, sharing the risks and successes with you."

That's what you call risk sharing. Taking an active interest in the client and assuming their issues and opportunities as your own. And vice versa. Again, symbiosis. Share the goal, the dream, the passion about doing something great together.

HOW TO AVOID ACCIDENTAL PARTNERSHIPS

In an e-learning partnership, as in any business alliance, it's the core purpose that matters, not the process, or partnering for the sake of partnership. Although this point may seem obvious on the surface, many businesses today really do partner for partnership's sake. Hey, let's partner? Hey, let's get married. *Think first.*

Why the partnering frenzy? Because partnering is "hot"—especially in e-learning. Organizations new to the concept, or those without considerable internal expertise, often ally themselves with content providers, infrastructure vendors, or services companies only to find themselves dancing with different partners long before the music stops.

> "It's a feeding frenzy."
>
> —Steve McMillen, vice president of learning, Hillenbrand Industries

So, do you have great partnerships? The first step is to go back to the beginning. Who are you as an organization and focus on the learner? What is the purpose? What is the passion? What are your strengths? What's at stake?

Next, look carefully at possible partners. What value do they really bring? What are their values? What will the "dance" be like? Partnerships are relationships, not transactions. Is that an organization you trust, enjoy working with, respect? Can their dreams and capacities blend with yours?

The next step is *key* and is usually missed. What if we invited you to a ballet or symphony that hadn't had any rehearsal? (We think you'd pass.) Imagine a football team making it to the Super Bowl without endless hours of practice. In business we race from "Let's partner!" to expecting great performances and end up disappointed at the dissidence. You gotta date. Take the time to understand how to work together.

John knows that when he calls Heather he will hear stories of the children's day and at some point talk to Bianca and hear her first-grade adventures. Heather enjoys hearing stories of John's workout schedule and his puppy's newest chewing adventure. It's part of writing the book. We understand when there is a crash in the background and the phone abruptly disconnects. We know the partnership is intact and that soon the phone will ring with the story and we will move onto the next chapter.

Rehearsal

Yes, rehearsal. How are we going to work together? Do you read e-mail or prefer phone calls? Who else is involved in the approval process? What are the technology constraints? Who has rights to the content? These are all nifty questions to ask up front, not in the middle.

When everything is working and you are practicing the protocols and Carson's advice from this chapter's case study, things go well. In every partnership there are challenges. Management shifts. Technology changes. Budgets go away. Deadlines change. People get jealous. The market slides. Hang on to your protocols, and a stronger partnership can develop.

So often people are in pain in their partnership. Go back to the focus of why are we here to begin with and explore which of the protocols may be out of whack. Sometimes you can make the revived partnership soar. If it really has gone sour, however, it is time to get out. As the song goes, "You gotta know when to hold 'em, know when to fold 'em, know when to walk away, and know when to run."

HOW TO AVOID PORCUPINE PARTNERSHIPS

Porcupine partnerships, as the name implies, are those alliances that are all quills and needles. They often begin with great promise only to become prickly, problematic, and just plain painful. Although the product or service supplied may be needed, and the potential is so . . . so full of *potential,* the agony of dealing with the vendor or people involved outweighs the pleasure. Or profit.

Accidental partnerships are one thing (they can even be fun and productive at first), but the porcupine variety is simply more trouble than it's worth. Hence, the name.

A common example, according to Richard Lozeau, CLO of ThinQ Learning Solutions, is a client who openly distrusts a vendor/partner. "One reason is that the buying public and training organizations haven't had much experience with high-tech hardware or software. A lot of education has to happen regarding how to make these kinds of decisions. As a result, it's very easy to fall into an adversarial conversation or relationship, in which the client distrusts the vendor or partner."

The irony is, as Lozeau and dozens of others interviewed point out, most vendors honestly only want success for their client/partners. "We need to engage in open, honest, frank conversations," adds Lozeau, "but they don't have to be adversarial. If they are—and continue along that vein for very long—a porcupine partnership will result. Both sides bristle; no one gets close."

Lozeau advises both vendors and clients to avoid porcupine partnerships by "following your own intuition. You have to be able to trust the people you're working with, but remember the old Reagan era slogan: 'Trust but verify.' I think some good questions a client needs to ask his or her vendor/partner at the outset are 'Who are your OEM suppliers? Whose code is embedded in your programs?'"

Elliott Masie, CEO of the Masie Institute, agrees. "I wish that some of the vendors would make my job easier by stating right up front that their products were inferior. I would have deep respect for their honesty and praise for the time they saved me in the evaluation process. But companies like that would not last very long.

"Still, I wish some of the vendors would answer a single question I have. It is an *answerable* question and would help them in the market. And it's simply this: 'What are the situations in which your product does not work?'

"After all, restaurants tell you up front if crabs are not in season or that a certain dish is only for people with a taste for spicy foods. Clothiers tell us that a certain dress will look best on someone with a *slightly different* figure. There are ways to deliver this news without sending the customer running out the door to a competitor. In fact, the desire to find the *best fit between the learner and the learning product* will almost always result in a positive vendor relationship" (our emphasis).

Here are a few more questions from Elliott's Vendor Sorting Question List:

- "Can I call a customer with the letter *S* at the start of their name for a reference?" This question will help you get comments from average customers, not just the fan club.

- "How long is the half-life of this technology or product?" In other words, how soon will there be an upgrade, revision, or change? And what happens to my investment then?

- "What are other developments that might impact the use of your technology?" Ask them to be honest about other emerging technologies and how they might replace or impact the product under consideration.

- "What is the learning philosophy of this product?" This may be a bit unfair to ask pure salespeople, but training vendors are in the training business and should be able to talk training to their customers. If you encounter a salesperson who is thrown by this query, ask to speak to someone on the training or development staff.

- "Who are your primary competitors?" Masie claims his wife asks this question whenever pitched by training vendors. Cathy Masie wants to hear their view of the marketplace and see whether they can articulate the difference between their products and others. If they say there aren't any competitors, use the old eyebrow raise.

Passion

Above all else, the solid, bedrock foundation of a successful partnership is *passion.*

Passion. Those who come soaring from the heart spark passion in others; it's reciprocal. Once a partnership has a shared vision—whether it's content author and client or multimedia guru and network administrator—real passion for perfection can result. "Until one is fully committed," says W. H. Murray, in *The Scottish Himalayan Expedition,* "there is hesitancy, the chance to draw back. The moment one definitely commits oneself, then Providence moves, too. All sorts of things occur to help one that would never otherwise have occurred."[2]

That's why we leave you with this final tip on e-learning partnerships, whatever their form or function: you must have *passion.* Shared vision. Total commitment.

Passion builds a relationship platform that raises everyone to a higher level. People may be instructed by reason, but they are inspired by passion.

What Works

- Trust your gut and keep your head.
- Know your partner.
- It's combining mutual strengths, not weaknesses.
- Beware of being bamboozled.
- Don't forget to rehearse.
- Essentials are honesty and trust.
- It's relationship, relationship, relationship.

Epilogue: What to Do Now?

Have no fear of perfection; you will never reach it.
—Salvador Dali

WHAT WORKS FOR YOU

As we stated at the outset, this book is a snapshot of e-learning as it is evolving today. It's not a perfect, all-inclusive compendium, be-all or end-all. We've outlined the steps necessary for finding the dance floor and tuning the orchestra: assessing, identifying, delegating, creating, and partnering. And remember, e-learning is an art, not a science. So, enjoy the great performance. Today.

But where is e-learning going? And how far will it take you or your organization?

We honestly don't know. No one does. It's still anyone's guess. We do know it is here to stay and will continue to change the way we learn or think about learning.

> "Online continuing education is creating a new and distinct educational realm, and it is the future of education."
> —Peter Drucker

One thing is certain—e-learning will evolve into something so simple, so eloquent yet all-pervasive and natural, that our grandchildren will wonder with dismay why we didn't see it coming. We believe that Wayne Hodgins, Marcia Conner, Jay Cross, and a host of others in the field are correct when they say that we're just watching this universe form. It will cool and coalesce to become so much a part of our everyday lives, we won't even think of it as a separate facet of work or play. It'll simply be how we do things. Just ask Heather's children who already live and learn on the Internet. (You mean there was a time when you didn't use computers to learn?) Online learning will become part of the everyday work experience—learning as a part of working.

We started this book during the height of the e-learning craze. Already the sizzle has mellowed to a slow boil. The title shifted from "e-learning" strategies to "online training." By the time you read these words, it might just be "e-work" or "working online." What we discerned during these turbulent times in our history, economy, and Internet growth and groans was that the fundamentals of "what works" stayed the same. One more time before we leave our time together: remember the learner.

During the good times or bad, whether training is blended, shaken, or stirred, cater to the learner. Period. If learners don't come or stayed tuned in, the rest doesn't matter, does it? So, focus less on proving what they learned and more on the evolution of whether they use it to begin with. We've all seen good intentions and poor execution.

Another recurring theme we have encountered while writing this book is the number of projects that have started and stop. (We can't tell you how many individual courses we have abandoned because of poor design or technical problems.) Having said that, we have also seen remarkable transitions at companies like Cisco and IBM that have made e-learning a part of the daily quilt of corporate knowledge.

As Tom Kelly, of Cisco, notes, "Learning is communicating; and e-learning is e-communicating." Avoid thinking of e-learning as equal to e-training. It is education, information, and communication. It's part of real knowledge management. Focus on and address business issues not training problems. It becomes integrated into the fabric of our daily work." This kind of experience requires corporate buy-in and understanding. Whether it is enabling people to take individual courses at their computer at home or in the office or participating in a global training program, e-learning needs to become a part of the new world of work.

The next generations will tap into e-learning with mystifying typing speed. For those of us who rely on pencils, we still have a way to go. Managers will learn the technology or have a career crash. At the same time, the folks creating all this wonderful stuff need to bring us along and assure we can use the information.

Consider this telling tale: Heather's six-year-old daughter was taught never to talk to strangers. After an uplifting learning experience with pride, she repeated what not to do if she encounters a stranger. Unfortunately, when asked what a stranger was, she didn't know. When launching people into the land of e, be sure the technology supports the learning and the learner.

Design? What does it mean to you? By now, we hope you'll consider replying, "What are they talking about? Learning design? Technical design? Graphic design? Or, *e-gads*, yes, all three!"

This is the strategy that most people struggle with. It's simple, and the answer lies in what is the best approach for the learning audience. So, at the risk of being redundant, please include all three design brains throughout the project. It will make a difference.

Global. Global. Global. It is a part of our corporate life. Whatever you are planning or pursuing, think about its global implications. Think again. Ask someone who is there. One of our clients designed a wonderful program that was tailored to a certain marketplace. What they discovered as they were rolling the program out was that some of the local offices didn't have access to the Internet. Oops. Many had only one computer for multiple groups of people. Keep learning. And think.

The evolution of e-learning will continue to involve partnerships—internally and externally. Remember that partnerships are about combining *strengths* for mutual benefit. Be clear on your strengths and what you need from a strong partner. Do your groundwork ahead of time to ensure that you have the same goals or dreams and that you develop a relationship that will sustain and grow the partnership and the project.

It is about continuous learning for those of us voyaging to this evolving, revolving world of online learning. Have fun. Learn lots. Try again. It is the future of education.

E-LEARNING ISN'T THE NEXT BIG THING—IT'S THE *NOW* BIG THING

When Heather was president of Tom Peter's training firm, Tom gave her the following strategic planning advice: "Just don't be boring."

Similarly, Boyd Clarke, CEO of the tompeters! company, is adamant about wowing your organization by taking action now. "Training ought to be a strategic intervention," says Clarke. "There's no time to train on miscellaneous objects or take an entire course just to learn one task. E-learning should be related to the core strategic intent of the company or skills you simply have to have. But what we're tending to do is put up a thousand courses, then say we're a university open for business. People show up, the content's not that great, then we test them on competencies that aren't all that important.

"My worst nightmare," Clarke adds, "is what we're going to do is get everybody in the nation to focus on what they're bad at and then measure it. Let's just shoot the whole industry in the foot right out of the bag. Most of the big name players are trying to measure everything, undoubtedly to assign some kind of ROI to e-learning. I say, just get it out of the box and start using it."

Remember, E-learning Is an Art, Not a Science

Roger McNamee, of Integral Capital Partners: "I look to the future of the Internet with only two firm convictions: (1) there is no limit to what the Internet can become over the next twenty years, and (2) I have no ability to predict how the Internet will turn out. The Internet eliminates barriers of distance, time and even politics. . . . With time, the 'Net should allow ideas and values to flow in all directions . . .

giving us access to the best of everything. Near term, I expect a consolidation period of two to five years, during which the bits and pieces of Internet infrastructure will evolve and stabilize, before finally becoming a truly solid platform for applications, content, and commerce."

We hope this book has helped you steer your way through the Internet jungle of jargon, Web weirdness, and e-everything. And we hope you'll use this book as it was intended—to help you understand, embrace, and use e-learning in the most efficient and effective way possible for your company, school, organization, and, above all, yourself to access life's knowledge.

> "The two great equalizers in life are the Internet and education."
> —JOHN CHAMBERS, CEO, Cisco

As we said when we began, nothing is the same as before. Old technologies are changing; classroom walls are rearranging. As Jay Cross puts it so well, "The 'Net changes everything."

Or, the way we see it, the net of online learning *that works* is a net-net benefit for everyone, everywhere.

Endnotes

INTRODUCTION

1. Quoted at www.idc.com/2000.
2. Ibid.
3. IntelliQuest, *Future of elearning* (1997). Internet Usage Survey data by IntelliQuest Information Group, a market research firm, also found the following results:
   - Most people in the United States access the Internet from home, followed by work and school (22 million from home, 13.3 million from work, 6.8 million from school).
   - The fastest-growing user age group is twenty-five to thirty-four years old, representing about 30 percent of all U.S. online users.
   - The Internet gender gap is shrinking: 45 percent of U.S. users are female.
   - The most commonly used Internet services are e-mail and information retrieval about hobbies, products, and services.
4. Brandon Hall (www.brandon-hall.com), newsletter, Spring 2001.
5. W. R. Hambrecht and Co., "What Wall Street Thinks and Why You Should Care," report, October 2001.

CHAPTER 1

1. Elliott Masie, *TechLearn* newsletter (Summer 2000), www.masie.com.
2. Alvin Toffler, *The Third Wave* (New York: Morrow, 1980).
3. Jay Cross, "E-learning," www.internettime.com, InternetTime Group, 2000.
4. Tony O'Driscoll, *Achieving Desired Business Performance* (International Society for Performance Improvement, 1999).
5. Marc Rosenberg, *Elearning: Strategies for Delivering Knowledge in the Digital Age* (New York: McGraw-Hill, 2000).
6. Samantha Chapnick, "Needs Assessment," www.researchdog.com, 2001.
7. Marcia Conner, "Adult Learning," www.learnativity.com, 2000.
8. Ibid.
9. The Institute for Learning Styles Research, www.learningstyles.org, 1999.
10. G. Millbank, paper presented at the Writers' Retreat on Interactive Technology and Equipment, Vancouver, Canada, 1994.
11. Claire Belilos, "Demystifying Training Design: Writing Training Objectives," www.eastytrain.com, 2001.
12. Lisa Collins, "Matching Content to Delivery? Remember the Basics," *Learning Circuits* (December 2000).

13. Conner, "Adult Learning." *Pedagogy* comes from the Greek word *paid*, meaning "child," and *agogus*, meaning "leader of."
14. Toffler, *The Third Wave*, 48.
15. Cross, "E-Learning."
16. Eduard C. Lindeman, *The Meaning of Adult Education* (New York: New Republic, 1989 [1926]).
17. Malcolm Knowles, *The Adult Learner: A Neglected Species* (New York: Gulf, 1998 [1973]).
18. Heather MacPherson, "Synchronous versus Asynchronous Delivery," unpublished manuscript, 2000.

CHAPTER 2
1. Matt Wetzel, "Stuck in the Middle," *Online Learning* (February 2001).
2. Stephen Griffin, as quoted by Bryan Chapman, "Through the Eyes of Visionaries," www.itimegroup.com/elearning.htm, 1999.
3. Brandon Hall, "Return on Investment and Multimedia Training," www.brandon-hall.com, 1999.
4. Jay Cross, "A Fresh Look at ROI," *Learning Circuits* (January 2001).
5. Hall, "Return on Investment and Multimedia Training."
6. Suzanne Biegel, as quoted by Wetzel, "Stuck in the Middle."
7. Stu Tanquist, as quoted by Wetzel, "Stuck in the Middle."
8. Brandon Hall and Jacques LeCavalier, "The Benchmarking Study of Best Practices: E-Learning across the Enterprise," www.brandon-hall.com, 2000.

CHAPTER 3
1. Brandon Hall and Jacques LeCavalier, "The Benchmarking Study of Best Practices: E-learning across the Enterprise," www.brandon-hall.com, 2000.
2. Ibid.
3. International Data Corporation, August 2001.
4. Samantha Chapnick, *Learning Circuits* (Summer 2001).
5. Ibid.
6. Ibid.
7. John Berry, "Corporate Training: The E-learning Factor," *Learning Circuits* (November 2000).
8. Clark Aldrich, as quoted by Berry, "Corporate Training."
9. Douglas Stefanko, as quoted by Berry, "Corporate Training."
10. Ibid.
11. Elizabeth Williams, as quoted by Berry, "Corporate Training."
12. Roy L. Karon, "Money Watch: Georgia Bank Finds Solutions in E-training," *eLearning Magazine* (March 2000).
13. Christine Pope, as quoted by Berry, "Corporate Training."
14. Jay Cross, www.internettime.com, 2000.
15. Ibid.
16. Mike Lynd, "Case in Point—Remote Classroom Training: An Economical Training Alternative for the FAA," *eLearning Magazine* (May 2000).
17. Quoted at http://www.india-future.com.
18. Cross, www.internettime.com.

CHAPTER 4
1. Glenn Rifkin, "Buckman Labs Is Nothing but Net," *Fast Company* (June 1996).
2. Christina Novicki, "Getting Started," *Fast Company* (June 1996).
3. M. Weil and L. Rosen, "How User Psychology Makes Technology Projects Fail," *HDSAware!* (online magazine of Hitachi Data Systems),1998.
4. Donald Norman, *Defending Human Attributes in the Age of the Machine* (CD-ROM), 1999.
5. Weil and Rosen, "How User Psychology Makes Technology Projects Fail."
6. Robert Heverly, "Training Helps Employees Overcome Technophobia," Capital District Business Reviews: Focus, *In-Depth: Office Quarterly* (July 10, 1998).
7. Distilled from Linda Puetz, "12 Learning Interventions That Combat Technophobia," *Learning Circuits* (March 2000).
8. Courtesy of Nua.com—www.nua.ie/surveys/how_many_online/index. html.
9. D. Hayes, "Technophobia? Fear Not!" *Kansas City Star* (June 1997).
10. Elliott Masie and Mark Van Buren, "If We Build It, Will They Come?" Learning Technology Acceptance Study, American Society for Training and Development, May 2001.
11. Ibid.

CHAPTER 5
1. Brad Grimes, "Taking E-learning to the Bank," © 2000 Cisco Systems, Inc.
2. Quoted by www.Roper.com/FYI.
3. *Encyclopedia of Education Technology,* ed. Bob Hoffman, Department of Educational Technology, San Diego State University, http://coe.sdsu. edu/eet.
4. Kevin Kruse, "Effective User Interface Design: The Four Rules," *Learning Circuits* (June 2000).
5. Ibid.
6. Distilled from Greg Willmarth, "Developing Multimedia for Low-End Hardware," *Learning Circuits* (February 2000).
7. Tony O'Driscoll, "What's Your Web-Based Learning Strategy?" *Learning Circuits* (February 2000).
8. Environmental Protection Agency, 1999.
9. From Ahlee Vance, "US Government Uses P2P to Share Data," IDG News Service, 2001.
10. Graphics courtesy of Cisco, 2000.
11. Patty Shank, "Open Sesame," *Learning Circuits* (April 2001).

CHAPTER 6
1. Quoted by www.Emarketer.com.
2. Donna J. Abernathy, "Global E-warming," *Learning Circuits* (May 2001).
3. Quoted at www.europa.eu.int/comm/education/life/index.html.
4. Quoted by Karen Birchard, "European Commission Adopts $13.3-Billion Plan That Is Expected to Promote Online Education," *The Chronicle of Higher Education: Daily News* (April 2001).
5. Ibid.

6. Reported on "Online Boost for Computer Skills," *BBC News Online* (June 2000).
7. Mary Gotschall, "E-learning," special section, *Fortune* (March 2001).
8. Stephen Alessi and Stanley Trollip, *Multimedia for Learning: Methods and Development* (Needham Heights, MA: Allyn & Bacon, 2001).
9. Carolyn Sostrom, "Localization: First Impressions Speak Volumes," *J@pan, Inc.* (May 2001).
10. Ibid.
11. Distilled from Carolyn Sostrom, "Tips for Localization Success," *J@pan, Inc.* (May 2001).

CHAPTER 7
1. Chip Bell and Heather Shea, "Protocols of Great Partnerships," an article based on their book *Dance Lessons: Six Steps to Great Partnerships in Business and Life* (San Francisco: Berrett-Koehler, 1998).
2. W. H. Murray, *The Scottish Himalayan Expedition* (London: Dent, 1951); quoted at www.doitnow.org/jpg/432doitnow.jpg.

Bibliography

BOOKS

Alessi, Stephen M., and Stanley R. Trollip. *Multimedia for Learning: Methods and Development.* Needham Heights, MA: Allyn & Bacon, 2001.

Bell, Chip, and Heather Shea. *Dance Lessons: Six Steps to Great Partnerships in Business and Life.* San Francisco: Berrett-Koehler, 1998.

Guffey, Mary Ellen. *Business Communications: Process and Product.* Cincinnati, OH: South-Western College Publishing, 2000.

O'Driscoll, Tony. *Achieving Desired Business Performance.* Washington, D.C.: International Society for Performance Improvement, 1999.

Rosenberg, Marc. *E-learning: Strategies for Delivering Knowledge in the Digital Age.* New York: McGraw-Hill, 2001.

REPORTS

Chandler, Dalton, and May Tang. *Education and E-learning: The Next Revolution.* New York: Needham, 2000.

Herman, Jerry, Robert Craig, and Leigh Pollak. *The E-education Industry.* Cleveland, OH: First Union Securities, 2000.

Ruttenbur, Brian, Ginger Spickler, and Sebastian Lurie. *E-learning: The Engine of the Knowledge Economy.* New York: Morgan Keegan, 2000.

Weggen, Cornelia, Keith Bachman, and Trace Urdan. *Corporate E-learning: Exploring a New Frontier.* San Francisco: Hambrecht, 2000.

MAGAZINE ARTICLES

Aldrich, Clark. "An Open Mind." *Online Learning* (May 2001): 66–67.

———. "Wither the Ivied Walls?" *Online Learning* (June 2001): 50–52.

Dobbs, Kevin. "What Price Is Right?" *Online Learning* (March 2001): 24–28.

Jones, Chris. "Rules of the Game." *Online Learning* (June 2001): 21–25.

Raths, David. "Measure of Success." *Online Learning* (May 2001): 20–26.

Sitze, Amy. "Land of Confusion." *Online Learning* (September 2001): 24–28.

INTERVIEWS

The following is a complete list of our interviewees, representing a broad spectrum of talents, roles, insights, and opinions in the field of online learning today. Again, wherever we have quoted someone not sourced in the endnotes, the information came from those interviewed.

Amy Seitz, editor in chief, *Online Learning* magazine

Bill Bandrowski and staff, CTC and Train2.com

Boyd Clark, CEO, tompeters! company

Claire Belilos, president, CHIC Hospitality Consulting Services

Clark Aldrich, VP e-learning, SimuLearn
Cliff and Debbie Dickinson, Instructional Dimensions
Conny Weggen, senior analyst, WRHambrecht and Co.
Dave Fallon, president, Integrity E-learning
Donald Norman, president, UNext Learning Systems
Carol Redfield, assistant director of computer science, St. Mary's University
Elliot Masie, CEO, Masie Institute
Eric Davis, general manager, Learn2.com
Eric Jenson, director of learning technologies, Marriott Inns
Grant Rickets, CEO, Saba
James Mosel, VP sales, Spectrum Industries, Inc.
Jason Chung, account executive, Learning Stream
Jay Cross, e-learning consultant, president, Internet Time Group, Inc.
Jennifer Hoffmann, Synergy Systems
Jim O'Hearn VP training, Marriott Inns
Keith Gallagher, publisher, *eLearning* magazine
Keith Hazen, Claire Favro, and Rebecca Bodrero, CTC
Kevin Oakes, president, Click2Learn
Marcia Conner, Learnativity
Mark Turner, manager, Strategic Alliances, GPe
Mary Beth Lamb and Peter Bailey, Wilson Learning's Global Solutions Group
Paul Earl, CEO Interactive Training, Inc.
Peg Maddocks and Chuck Barritt, Cisco Systems
Peter Hackes, founder and president, Learning Stream
Robert Wilkins, e-learning consultant, PricewaterhouseCoopers
Ron Zemke, editor in chief, *Training* magazine
Samantha Chapnick, CEO, Research Dog
Scott Sutker and Patsy Linker, First Union Bank
Steve McMillen, vice president of executive leadership development, Hillen-
    brand Industries
Steven Smith, account executive, 27/7 University
Sarah and Doug Sudheer, Click2Learn
Suley Usman, president/CEO, PeakQuest
Tom Kelly, vice president of E-learning, Cisco Systems
Tony O'Driscoll, executive-in-residence, IBM
Wayne Hodges, strategic futurist, Auto Desk
William Shea, manager, Harvard Business School Publishing

Glossary

Now comes the part you've all been waiting for—a clue to all those delightful terms and acronyms you find scattered about the Internet. Yes, the same ones you must muddle through whenever talking to an IT person, e-learning vendor, or some other tech type. "Our ASP can handle your RLOs, provided they're built around ADL's SCORM or AICC—unless you're using CLEO or IMS, in which case your RIOs could be SOL, Q.E.D. Ipso facto, ad nauseam, EIEIO."

We now present our Glossary of Terms *and* IOIA (Interpretation of Internet Acronyms). Like most everything in this book, the times and buzzwords they are a-changing, and new ones have been added and some deleted, but here goes. Our thanks to CNET, ZDNET, and Eva Kaplan-Leiserson of ASTD. (ASTD's e-learning Webzine, *Learning Circuits,* offers an e-learning glossary with more than 275 terms. Updated monthly, the glossary is reviewed and certified by a panel of e-learning experts. It's also available in Spanish.)

10BaseT: The most common form of Ethernet is called 10BaseT, which denotes a peak transmission speed of 10 mbps using copper twisted-pair cable. Ethernet is a standard for connecting computers into a local area network (LAN).

100BaseT: Another term for fast Ethernet, an upgraded standard for connecting computers into a local area network (LAN). 100BaseT Ethernet works just like regular Ethernet except that it can transfer data at a peak rate of 100 mbps. It's also more expensive and less common than its slower 10BaseT sibling.

24/7: Twenty-four hours a day, seven days a week. In e-learning, this term is used to describe the hours of operation of a virtual classroom or how often technical support should be available for online students and instructors.

A

ACK (acknowledgment): When a modem receives a data packet, it sends a signal back to the sending modem. If all the data are present and correct, it sends an ACK signal, which acts as a request for the next data packet. If the modem didn't get all the data, it sends back a negative acknowledgment, or NAK.

ADL (Advanced Distributed Learning): An initiative by the U.S. Department of Defense to standardize computer and Internet-based learning software by developing a common framework, based on XML and other coding languages, which contains content in the form of reusable learning objects. See also SCORM and the ADL Web site.

ADSL (asymmetric digital subscriber line): A type of DSL that uses standard phone lines to deliver high-speed data communications. Unlike ISDNs, whose transmission speed is limited to 64 kbps, ADSL technology can deliver upstream (from the user) speeds up to 640 kbps and downstream (to the user) speeds of more than 6 mbps. Plus, ADSL only uses the portion of a phone line's bandwidth not utilized by voice, allowing for simultaneous voice and data transmission.

AGP (accelerated graphics port): A graphics bus slot on PC motherboards designed to transfer graphics data at rates up to 528 megabytes/second. Greater speed lets game and 3D applications store and retrieve larger, more realistic textures in system memory rather than video memory, thus avoiding performance hits.

AICC: Aviation Industry Computer-Based Training Committee, the leading international association of technology-based training professionals that develops training guidelines for the aviation industry.

Amplitude: The variety in a signal. Commonly thought of as the *height of a wave.*

Analog: A signal received in the same form as it was transmitted, though the frequency and amplitude may vary.

ANSI (American National Standards Institute): An organization of American industry groups that works internationally to develop standards that facilitate international trade and telecommunications. Some of ANSI's greatest achievements include ASCII, SCSI, and the ANSI.SYS device driver.

ASCII (American Standard Code for Information Interchange): Pronounced "askee." A text standard developed by ANSI to define how computers write and read characters. The ASCII set of 128 characters includes letters, numbers, punctuation, and control codes. Most operating systems use the ASCII standard, except for Windows NT, which uses the Unicode standard.

ASP (application service provider): Third-party firms that manage and distribute software-based services (e-commerce, e-learning) to companies over the Internet from a central location. Companies save money, time, and network resources by outsourcing some or all of their IT needs via ASPs.

Asynchronous: Communication in which interaction between parties does not take place simultaneously.

ATM (asynchronous transmission mode): A method of sending data in irregular time intervals using a code such as ASCII. ATM allows most modern computers to communicate with one another easily.

Audio bridge: A device used in audioconferencing that connects multiple telephone lines.

Audioconferencing: A voice-only connection of more than two sites using standard telephone lines.

B

Backbone: A main communication path in a network connecting multiple users.

Band: A range of frequencies within one defined spectrum.

Bandwidth: The amount of information a communication channel can carry.

Binary: A computer language developed with only two digits in its alphabet (0s and 1s).

BIOS (bit input/output system): Set of instructions coded into a PC's ROM to control system hardware. Both the main operating system (OS) and application programs access BIOS routines to provide compatibility for such functions as screen display and boot-up sequence.

Bit: Abbreviation for a single binary digit (1-0).

Bps (bits per second): A measurement of a modem's data transmission speed. Also called "baud rate."

Browser: Software that allows you to find and see information on the Internet, including multimedia streaming audio/video.

Byte: A single computer word, generally eight bits.

C

CAI (computer-assisted instruction): Instruction refereed by a computer, which allows for slight alterations based on student answers but not for changes in the overall program structure.

CBT (computer-based training): Educational material presented on a computer, primarily via CD-ROM or floppy disk. Unlike Web-based training, CBT doesn't require a network connection and typically doesn't provide links to learning resources outside of the course.

CD-ROM (compact disc read-only memory, or compact disc read-only media): A computer storage medium, similar to an audio CD, that can hold over seven hundred megabytes of read-only digital information.

Central processing unit (CPU): The component of a computer in which data processing takes place.

Channel: The smallest subdivision of a circuit, usually with a path in only one direction.

CMOS (complementary metal-oxide semiconductor): A low-power semiconductor chip used in PCs to hold basic start-up information (e.g., the time and date) and used in turn by the system's BIOS.

CMS (content management system): Software application that streamlines the process of designing, testing, approving, and posting e-learning modules, content or Web pages. Similar to a Learning Management System (see LMS), but focused more on actual content than system management.

CoD (Content on demand): Delivery of an offering, packaged in a media format, anywhere, anytime via a network. Variants include audio on demand (AoD) and video on demand (VoD).

Codec (COder/DECoder): Device used to convert analog signals to digital signals for transmission and reconvert signals upon reception at the remote site while allowing for the signal to be compressed for less expensive transmission.

COM port (communications port): Used to describe the serial port on a PC that allows interaction between the motherboard and an input device (modem, mouse, etc.). Typically associated with a number, as in COM1, COM2, COM3, or COM4.

Compressed video: When video signals are downsized to allow travel along a smaller carrier.

Compression: Reducing the amount of visual information sent in a signal by only transmitting changes in action.

Computer-assisted instruction (CAI): Teaching process in which a computer is utilized to enhance the learning environment by assisting students in gaining mastery over a specific skill.

CPU (central processing unit): The brain of any computer—the main processing chip that takes "requests" from applications and performs operations. The faster your processor, the more operations it can execute per second and the faster your applications can run. The term *CPU* is also used to describe the whole box that contains the chip, along with the motherboard, expansion cards, disk drives, power supply, and so forth. Both uses are common, but only the first is truly accurate.

CRM (customer relationship management): Programs, databases, and methods for helping a company manage and organize customer relationships.

Cyberspace: The nebulous "place" where humans interact over computer networks. Coined by William Gibson in *Neuromancer.*

D

Desktop videoconferencing: Videoconferencing on a personal computer.

Dial-up teleconference: Using public telephone lines for communications links among various locations.

Digital: An electrical signal that varies in discrete steps in voltage, frequency, amplitude, locations, and so on. Digital signals can be transmitted faster and more accurately than analog signals.

Digital Video Interactive: See DVI.

Distance education: The process of providing instruction when students and instructors are separated by physical distance and technology, often in tandem with face-to-face communication, is used to bridge the gap.

Distance learning: The desired outcome of distance education.

Download: Using the network to transfer files from one computer to another.

DSL (digital subscriber line): Broadband Internet access method that sends data over standard phone lines at speeds up to 7 mbps. DSL is available to subscribers who live within a certain distance of the necessary router (usually no more than fifteen thousand feet).

DVD (digital versatile disc): Optical disks that are the same size as CDs but are double-sided and have larger storage capacities.

DVI (digital video interactive): A format for recording digital video onto compact disk allowing for compression and full-motion video.

E

Echo cancellation: The process of eliminating acoustic echo in a videoconferencing room.

Electronic mail (e-mail): Sending messages from one computer user to another.

EPSS (electronic performance support system): A computer application to another application so that, when accessed, it trains or guides workers through steps they need to complete a task in the target application. Or, a computer or other device that enables workers to access information or resources to help them achieve a task or performance requirements.

ERP (enterprise resource planning): A set of functions supported by application software to manage and streamline a company's core activities, such as product planning, parts purchasing, inventory management, order tracking, and customer service. Can also include modules for finance and HR activities.

F

F2F (face-to-face): Used to describe the traditional classroom environment (see also ILT).

Facsimile (fax): System used to transmit textual or graphical images over standard telephone lines.

FAQ (frequently asked questions): A file established for public discussion groups containing questions and answers new users often ask. Often used by OEMs and vendors to fob frustrated users off and avoid direct contact or customer service.

Fiber optic cable: Glass fiber that is used for laser transmission of video, audio, and/or data.

File Transfer Protocol (FTP): A protocol that allows you to move files from a distant computer to a local computer using a network like the Internet.

Frequency: The space between waves in a signal. The amount of time between waves passing a stationary point.

FTP: See File Transfer Protocol.

Full-motion video: A signal that allows transmission of complete action taking place at the origination site.

Fully interactive video: Two sites interact with audio and video as if they were co-located. Also known as *two-way interactive video.*

G

GB (gigabyte): Just over one billion bytes: 1,008 megabytes.

GIF (Graphics Interchange Format): File format developed by CompuServe to store images. GIFs support 256 colors and are often used for Web images because they compress well.

GUI (graphical user interface): Computer interface using icons or pictures, pull-down menus, and a mouse—for example, Macintosh and Windows.

H

HDTV (high-definition TV): Television that has over five times the resolution of standard television. Requires extraordinary bandwidth.

Home page: A document with an address (URL) on the World Wide Web maintained by a person or organization that contains pointers to other pieces of information.

Host: A network computer that can receive information from other computers.

Hyper Text Markup Language (html): The code used to create a home page and is used to access documents over the World Wide Web.

Hypertext: A document that has been marked up to allow a user to select words or pictures within the document, click on them, and connect to further information.

Hypertext Transfer Protocol (http): The protocol used to signify that an Internet site is a WWW site; that is, http is a WWW address.

I

IEEE: The Institute of Electrical and Electronics Engineers. Their Learning Technology Standards Committee is working to develop technical standards, recommended practices, and guides for computer implementations of education and training systems.

ILS (integrated learning system): A complete software, hardware, and network system used for instruction. In addition to providing curriculum and lessons organized by level, an ILS usually includes a number of tools such as assessments, record keeping, report writing, and user information files that help to identify learning needs, monitor progress, and maintain student records.

ILT (instructor-led training): Usually refers to traditional classroom training, where an instructor leads a roomful of students through lessons. The term is used synonymously with *on-site training* and *classroom training.*

IMS (Instructional Management System) Global Learning Consortium: A coalition of government organizations dedicated to defining and distributing open architecture interoperability specifications for e-learning products.

Instructional Television Fixed Service (ITFS): Microwave-based, high-frequency television used in educational program delivery.

Integrated Services Digital Network (ISDN): A telecommunications standard allowing communications channels to carry voice, video, and data simultaneously.

Interactive media: A frequency assignment that allows for a two-way interaction or exchange of information.

Internet: An international network of networks primarily used to connect education and research networks begun by the United States government.

Internet Protocol (IP): The international standard for addressing and sending data via the Internet.

IP: See Internet Protocol.

ISDN (Integrated Services Digital Network): Communications technology created in 1984 to allow wide-bandwidth digital transmission using the public switched telephone network. Under ISDN, a phone call can transfer sixty-four kilobits of digital data per second. Carries voice, video, and data simultaneously.

ISO: International Organization for Standardization, an international federation of national standards bodies. See the ISO Web site.

ISP (Internet service provider): A reseller of Internet access services.

ITFS (Instructional Television Fixed Service): Microwave-based, high-frequency television used in educational program delivery.

IT (information technology): Computers and their information processing capabilities.

J

Java: An *object-oriented* program language that allows Internet users to participate in interactive multimedia features (animation and calculation). Using small Java programs, called applets, Web pages can include multimedia features.

JDBC (Java Database Connectivity): An application program interface used to connect programs written in Java to the data in popular databases.

JPEG (Joint Photographic Experts Group): A standard for compressing digital photographic images.

K

KB (kilobyte): 1,024 bytes; often applied to 1,000 bytes as well.

Kbps (kilobytes per second): A measurement of data transmission speed.

KMS (knowledge management system): A software system for capturing, organizing, and storing knowledge and experiences of employees within an organization and making it available to others. The information is stored in a special database called a *knowledge base.*

L

LAN (local area network): A group of computers and other peripheral devices (i.e., servers, printers) located in a relatively limited area, which share information and can communicate with each other.

Listserv: An e-mail program that allows multiple computer users to connect onto a single system, creating an on-line discussion.

LMS (learning management system): Software that automates, administers, and tracks training. The LMS registers users, tracks courses in a catalog, and records data from learners; it also provides reports to management. Usually does not include authoring tools, instead focusing on managing courses created by others.

Local area network: See LAN.

LRN: Microsoft's Learning Resource Interchange, a format that gives content creators a standard way to identify, share, update, and create online content and courseware. LRN is the first commercial application of the IMS Content Packaging Specification.

LSP (learning service provider): A specialized ASP offering learning management and training delivery software on a hosted or rental basis.

M

MB (megabyte): 1,000,000 bytes.

Mbps (megabits per second): A million bits per second.

Microwaves: Electromagnetic waves that travel in a straight line and are used to and from satellites and for short distances (i.e., up to thirty miles).

Modem: A piece of equipment to allow computers to interact with each other via telephone lines by converting digital signals to analog for transmission along analog lines.

Mosaic: An example of browser software that allows WWW use.

MP3: A format for music file compression that allows users to download music over the Internet.

MPEG (Moving Picture Experts Group): A standard for compressing digital video images.

Multimedia: Any document that uses multiple forms of communication, such as text, audio, and/or video.

Multi-Point Control Unit (MCU): Computerized switching system that allows point-to-multipoint videoconferencing.

N

Netscape: An example of browser software that allows you to design a home page and to browse links on the WWW.

Network: A series of points connected by communication channels in different locations.

O

ODBC (Open Database Connectivity): An application program interface to access information from numerous types of databases, including Access, dbase, and DB2.

Online: Active and prepared for operation. Also suggests access to a computer network.

Origination site: The location from which a teleconference originates.

P

P2P: Peer-to-peer network connection, in which two client or "peer" computers exchange information with minimal server involvement. This was the heart of Napster.

PCI (Peripheral Component Interconnect): A self-configuring PC local bus designed by Intel to interface with a wide variety of additional peripheral devices (printers, modems, etc.) with increased performance. If you have a Pentium system, be sure any add-in board you buy is a PCI device.

PDA (personal digital assistant): Handheld computer device used to organize personal information such as phone numbers, schedules, and etc. Data can usually be transferred to a desktop computer by cable or wireless transmission.

POP (point of presence): The geographic location of a specific service or switch.

Point-to-point: Transmission between two locations.

Point-to-multipoint: Transmission between multiple locations using a bridge.

PPP: A software package that allows a user to have a direct connection to the Internet over a telephone line.

Protocol: A formal set of standards, rules, or formats for exchanging data that assures uniformity between computers and applications.

R

RAM (random-access memory): Temporary storage space for data and program instructions.

RIO (reusable information object): Pronounced "ree-oh." A single piece of content, practice, or assessment that can be grouped with other similar pieces to form a single learning objective. RIOs are the smallest chunk of learning that still has meaning for the learner.

RLO (reusable learning object): A collection of 7±2 RIOs, including overview, summary, and assessment, that supports a specific learning objective.

ROM (read-only memory): Storage chip containing noneditable instructions for use when a computer boots. The instructions, contained in a small program called the BIOS, load from ROM and start the hard disk so the operating system (OS) can be loaded and the user can begin. Some ROM chips can be updated with new BIOS instructions.

S

SCORM (Sharable Content Object Reference Model): Specifications for designing granular, reusable learning objects for use in course content. Developed by the Department of Defense's Advanced Distributed Learning (ADL) initiative, SCORM-compliant courseware is designed to interface with other compliant elements to produce a repository of reusable training materials.

SCSI (Small Computer System Interface): Pronounced "skuzzy." Hardware add-on standard first adopted by MacIntosh to allow up to seven additional devices to a computer (hard drives, CD-ROMs, etc.), which can handle single-interface issues. A robust standard, it was recently updated to SCSI-2.

Server: A computer with a special service function on a network, generally receiving and connecting incoming information traffic.

SLIP (Serial Line Internet Protocol): Allows a user to connect to the Internet directly over a high-speed modem.

Slow scan converter: Transmitter/receiver of still video over narrow band channels. In real time, camera subjects must remain still for highest resolution.

SME (subject-matter expert): An individual with proficient knowledge about and skills in a particular topic or subject area.

SOL: An off-color term meaning "completely out of luck." (Figure it out.)

SQL: A database standard employed primarily by Microsoft in its SQL Server product.

Synchronous: Communication in which interaction between participants is simultaneous.

T

T-1 (DS-1): High-speed digital data channel that is a high-volume carrier of voice and/or data. Often used for compressed video teleconferencing. T-1 has twenty-four voice channels.

T-3 (DS-3): A digital channel that communicates at an even faster rate than T-1.

TBT (technology-based training): The delivery of content via Internet, LAN or WAN, satellite broadcast, audio or video tape, interactive TV, or CD-ROM. Includes CBT and WBT.

TCP/IP: The protocol that allows data packet traffic over the Internet.

Telecommunication: The science of information transport using wire, radio, optical, or electromagnetic channels to transmit receive signals for voice or data communications using electrical means.

Teleconferencing: Two-way electronic communication between two or more groups in separate locations via audio, video, and/or computer systems.

Tetrabyte: One thousand gigabytes, or one million megabytes.

Transmission Control Protocol (TCP): A protocol that makes sure that packets of data are shipped and received in the intended order.

Transponder: A satellite transmitter and receiver that receives and amplifies a signal prior to retransmission to an Earth station.

U

Uplink: The communication link from the transmitting earth station to the satellite.

URL (Uniform Resource Locator): The address of a home page on the WWW. For example, http://www.bkpub.com = Berrett-Koehler Publishers' home page.

V

Video teleconferencing: A teleconference including two-way video.

VoD (video on demand): See CoD.

VOIP (voice over IP): Voice transmitted digitally using the Internet Protocol. Avoids fees charged by telephone companies.

VPN (virtual private network): A private network configured inside a public network.

W

W3C: World Wide Web Consortium, an organization developing interoperable specifications, software, and tools for the WWW. See the W3C Web site.

WAN (wide area network): A computer network that spans a relatively large area. Usually made up of two or more local area networks. The Internet is a WAN.

WAP (wireless application protocol): A specification that allows Internet content to be read by wireless devices.

WBT: Web-based training; synonymous with *e-learning*.

WML: Wireless Markup Language. An XML-based language that allows the text of Web pages to be displayed on cellular phones and personal digital assistants.

WWW (World Wide Web): A graphical hypertext-based Internet tool that provides access to home pages created by individuals, businesses, and other organizations.

X

XML (Extensible Markup Language): The next-generation HTML that will allow Web site designers to program their own markup commands. These commands can then be used throughout the Web site as if they were standard HTML commands.

Index

About the Authors

 **Heather Shea-Schultz** is a partner with the Canaan Consulting Group (CCG) and the former president of Tom Peters' training company. She was also the executive vice president of marketing for Learn2. An internationally recognized speaker and consultant, she brings computers to rural Kenya and installs them for a month each year. In addition, she is on the advisory board of Interactive Training, Inc. Heather is coauthor with Chip Bell of *Dance Lessons: Six Steps to Great Partnerships in Business and Life* (Berrett-Koehler, 1998).

John Fogarty is a published novelist, columnist, seasoned e-learning writer, and former stand-up comedian. He is the author of *The Haunt,* a novel published by Warner Books (1990). Since then, John has written four more novels of mystery and suspense and penned three motion picture screen-  plays, all sold to DreamLine Productions. A professional writer with over twenty-five years' experience, John is also a published poet and short story author. Certified in Human Performance Technology's Accomplishment-Based Curriculum Design by the Moore Institute, he has written extensively on the opportunities of the new economy and technology. He's also the "technical guy" of this writing team, one of those half-crazed e-fiends who create online learning modules and courses.